Tales from Tuckahoe
ISBN # 978-1-7350258-6-5
Copyright L. Clayton Cate 2021
Illustrations by the author.
Published by The Meadows Farm, Inc.
Willis, VA

Tales from Tuckahoe

Dedication

When I started writing stories of my memories of Tuckahoe, and posting them on Facebook, the people of Tuckahoe are the ones who enjoyed the stories I wrote, and who let me know they did. They are the people who urged me to publish my stories and poems, and they, the people of Tuckahoe, are the sole reason I decided to do it: not for fame, or for money,
but hopefully to spread a little Joy.
I love you guys and this book is for you.
I really hope you enjoy it.

This book is dedicated to the people of Tuckahoe, TN

TALES FROM TUCKAHOE

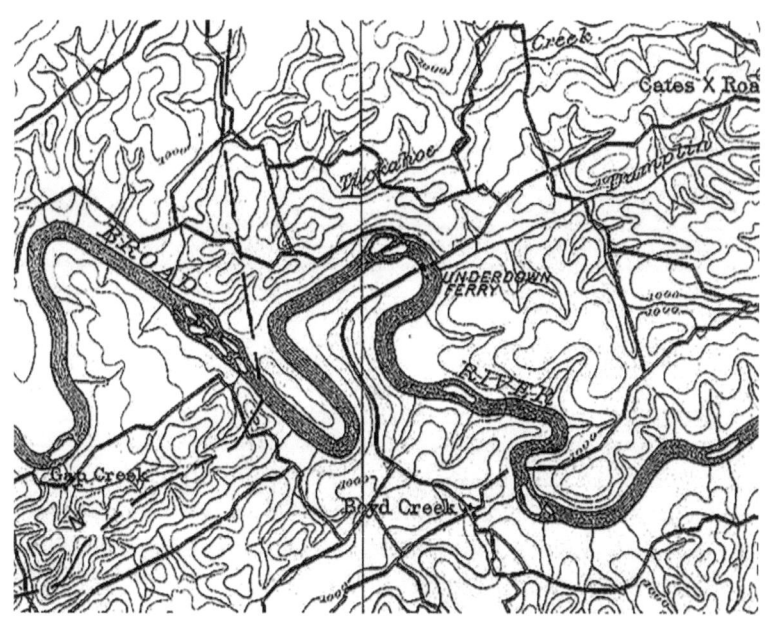

L. CLAYTON CATE

Table of Contents

Tuckahoe the Place

Tuckahoe Tennessee — 2

Tuckahoe the People

Drink'ng From the Spring — 10
The Fishers Seat — 12
The Tuckahoe Sand Ridges — 13
Tuckahoe Snapshots — 16
Willie's Shoulder Bone — 19
Veda Rocked Away — 21
Television Comes to Tuckahoe — 24
Tuckahoe and the H. H. Smith General Store — 27
Virgin Moon — 29
Raab-ben-hoe — 31
1940s, A Day at Smith School — 33

Hog Killing Day in Tuckahoe	38
Turning on the Light	43
Whittling	45
The Marble King of Smith School	47
A Day at the Movies, Somewhere around 1950	50
A Memory of Peaches	53

As Good as It Gets	55
Smith School and the Columbus Stockade Blues	57
Noble	60
Fox and Hound	62
On Going to Town from Tuckahoe	64
Of Elkins Road, and Wooden Wagons	67

Is That You?	71
John McFine	74
Do You Remember the Tuckahoe Dips?	76
Moving Day by Horse and Wagon, 1943	78
Cooperation	81
Youth's Wages	82
Emily Fair	84
Burnt Oil	86
Home Is	89
Rain Drop Lullaby	90
Love Can Come in A Box	91
The Rock Hole, A legendary place	93
Flooties and Boobies (flu-TIE's & BOO-bee's)	96
The Gardener's Shoes	99
The War with Sockless	101
Sadie, A True Dog Story	104
The Hiding Place	107
Attic Bed	109
River Time	110
Snow on the Tuckahoe Hills	112
Tuckahoe	114
Tuckahoe in the Winter	116

The Country Church

The Country Church	121
Mary's Door	122
Humble Pie	125
A Poor Man's House	127
Adam's Hand	129
Fires in the Wildwood	131
God's Gift	136
Such Is	138
Looking for You	139
If'n Jesus Wuz	141
A Little Short	143
Cause for Celebrat'ng?	144
Lazarus at the Gate	146
A Simple Man	154
Power in the Book	156

Farther Out

Wet Wood	160
I Am	161
Needful Things	162
Twilight World	163
Nature's brew	164
Wished Away	165
Bone of My Bone	167
What Love Is	168
A Lover's Touch	170
Of Interpretation	171
Near to Home	172
If You Think of Me	173
Sweet on Me	174
Mmmmm!	175
Papaw Blues	176
Disposable Love	178
Two Travelers	180
Usetabees	182
The News	183
Va—Room! Va—Room!	184
November's Wind	185
A Time of Leaving	187
More Than Enough	188
July	190
Christmas Present	191
An Unruly Visitor	192

Rambling

Bluet's	196
Out of Body	197
Forest Smoke	199
Spring Symphony	200
One Stormy Day	201
Creation's Voice	203
More dumplings	204
Conformity	205
Voyager	206

Undefeated	208
Troubles	209
Reflection	210
Poets Try	211
Barefoot Dream	212

If I Had Wings	213
The Tribal Council	214
No Farewell	215
Wreck on Turkey Pen Ridge	216
A Work Not Signed	217
Winsome Wind	219
Sail Away	221
The Evening and the Morning	223
Seeker of Fortune	224
Roses, Quilts, and Time	225
Westward Trek	226
Walking Softly	228
New Tenant	229
Only one	229
No One More Than Me	230
Where Blue Mountains Are	231
Go Out, Young Man!	232
The Cowboy Way	233

Tuckahoe the Place

Tuckahoe Tennessee

This book is about a place called Tuckahoe and the people who call that place home. Tuckahoe was the worst and best of places. Filled with creeks, rivers, woods fields, hills, and hollows. It was a good place for a boy to grow up.

Tuckahoe is located in the Tennessee Valley between the Holston and French Broad Rivers and was more a region than a community. Tuckahoe was one of those places without real boundaries as it embraced several communities but was generally comprised of the area defined by the watershed of the Tuckahoe creek; a long meandering stream that eventually emptied into the French Broad River about twenty miles above Knoxville. The several communities in Tuckahoe included: Thorn Grove; Midway; Paw Paw Hollow; and the area around Smith Store and Smith School.

How it came to be called by the name Tuckahoe had passed out of living memory. The name is not unique for there are at least 106 places in the eastern United States called Tuckahoe.

It would appear Tuckahoe is how the white man pronounced and spelled the Indian word "Tockawhoughe". It was the name of a marshland plant from whose root the Indians made a type of bread. I am thinking by the time we came along, the conditions favorable for that plant to grow here no longer existed, but that would make another story not told here. Nobody I ever met, who lived in my Tuckahoe, knew anything about that plant.

Tuckahoe must have been considered unfit for an Indian town or settlement and was used by the Indians primarily as a hunting ground. The evidence for thousands of years of hunting was the profusion of arrowheads sown over the area. They turned up in plowed fields and eroded gullies, and no doubt there was a story attached to every one of them because an Indian would certainly never have thrown one away.

You can almost imagine a white man walking through an uninhabited area with an Indian guide and happening upon a big creek. The Indian may have pointed to the creek and said "Tockahoughe". The white man takes out his rough map, draws in the creek, and jots down, "Tuckahoe Creek."

Around the year 1790, over from North Carolina, and down from Virginia, the white man began to creep into the lands west of the Appalachian Mountains. Some moved into the watershed of the Tuckahoe Creek. They found it an uninhabited place and claimed a piece of it for their own.

Beaver dams had converted many of the streams into marshland where the tuckahoe plant could no longer grow. One thing they learned, likely the hard way, was you couldn't live in the level bottoms of the creeks and rivers because they flooded often. They settled for the hill and ridge tops and built their houses there. At least that was so in the place we now call Tuckahoe, but the ridges were not all created equal in Tuckahoe.

If you drive through Tuckahoe today, you will not see a "Welcome to Tuckahoe" sign, nor a sign that says "You are now leaving Tuckahoe, come back to visit again soon". Nor will you find it on a map, for there is no place called Tuckahoe on any modern map of East Tennessee. But this book is not so much about the land, though it is an interesting area located in the beautiful, hilly, and well-watered Tennessee Valley. It is really about the people who live there, and maybe a little something about the people who lived here for thousands of years before we did.

There was once a Tuckahoe post office here a little over a hundred twenty-six years ago, located no doubt in a general store. I found that on an 1895 map of Knox County TN, in the 22nd District.

You can find Tuckahoe Creek on a map. It flows for 16 miles through Tuckahoe and empties into the French Broad River about 20 miles east of Knoxville. If you can locate the Tuckahoe Creek, you have found Tuckahoe.

I have a distant kin person, who, back in the 1930s, put registers in places where people would gather, such as church homecomings, decoration days, and family reunions, and she asked the guests to sign them, and to write down the names of fathers, mothers, and grandparents, as far back as they knew. Later she published a book, "Our East Tennessee Kinsmen" and using the records she compiled, the intermarriage of the families who lived in Tuckahoe can be easily made out.

Living in Tuckahoe was like being part of a large extended family. It was a place where everybody knew everybody for miles and miles around and were more than likely related to them; some distantly, some close, and some way too close. That place I knew is not gone, but it has changed. It was not a sudden change. It happened slowly and piece by piece. As the modern world came to our part of the valley the old ways were slowly replaced and the construction of Interstate 40, which split the area squarely in two, completed the transformation.

At the time of my birth in 1938, Tuckahoe was one of those backwater places that time had not forgotten about but had ignored. A place of gravel roads, no electricity, no telephones, no running water, and outdoor toilets. Going barefoot in the summer was accepted practice for everyone, young and old alike.

A granddaughter of Henry Smith, who owned our General store, delivered groceries for the store for a time, told me that she had eaten in every house on Elkins road, and came to love all those people. You cannot know what that means unless you live in Tuckahoe.

I look back in memory at my life in Tuckahoe, and perhaps especially at the time I begin to realize who I was, where I was, and who the others were I found myself living with. I call this waking up, and when I woke up, I found I lived on a ridge top in Tuckahoe, Tennessee. I was born in the house I woke up in. That old house no longer exists, and neither does the one I later grew up in.

I have learned that my Tuckahoe is a hard place to write about. In trying to do that, I find you need a wide brush to paint a picture of the people of Tuckahoe. Some few lived in the depth of poverty while others were successful farmers and businessmen. Some had not learned to read, and others had college educations and were school teachers. But they intermingled, they knew each other by name and got along well, and that is what made Tuckahoe a special place. In East Tennessee, it is the year of 2021 as I write this, and in the last 100 years, a lot has changed. In East Knox County, we now have a state park, a golf course, and a new business park that is under development. The golf course is called the Seven Islands Golf Course, the state park is called the State Birding Park, and the business park is called the Midway Business Park. There are high-scale subdivisions springing up along the river and small-scale estates are being built on the gentle slopes of the broad ridges. They all have something in common: they are all in Tuckahoe.

But this book is not so much about the land, though it is an interesting area located in the beautiful, hilly, and well-watered Tennessee Valley. It is really about the people who live there, and maybe a little something about the people who lived here for thousands of years before we did. I am writing this book for the people of Tuckahoe. They are good people, and they wanted me to publish my memories and poems about Tuckahoe. They are almost all friends of mine, and many are distant relatives. I love you guys, and this is for you. I hope you enjoy it.

And so begins my tales of Tuckahoe.

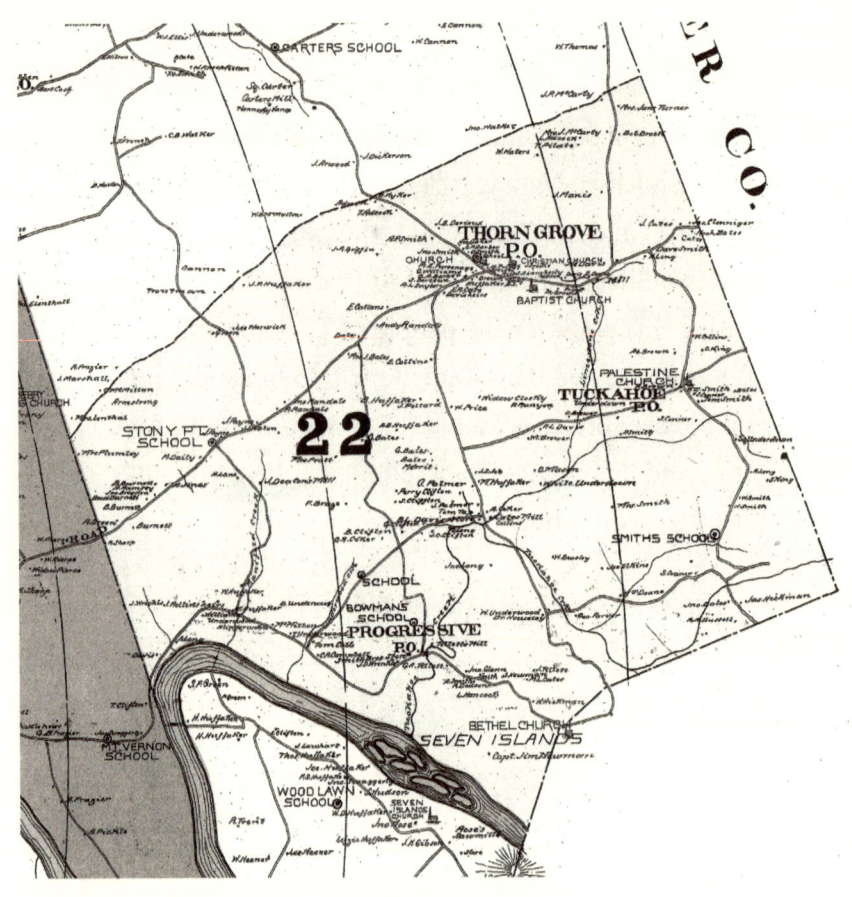

1895 Map of 22nd District, Knox County, Tennessee

TUCKAHOE THE PEOPLE

Drink'ng From the Spring

The morn'ng sun's proclaim'ng
That old wintertime is done,
As the trees and little bushes
Put their springtime britches on.

Many shades of green combin'ng
With a dab of pink and white,
And they shore look mighty purty
In the early morn'ng light.

With a choir of song birds raising
Hallelujahs to the year.
It's about the sweetest music
That a man will ever hear.

And they all are build'ng houses
While dividing up the trees.
And the smells from nature's kitchen
Is a call'ng to the bees.

The little creek has gotten sassy
Just warbling as it goes.
It got high up in the mountains
Sipping on the melt'ng snow.

And I'm stand'ng by the cabin
Just a drink'ng in the view,
From the wonder that's surround'ng,
I'm intoxicated, too.

The Fishers Seat

I see a sun high in the sky
        I see a day in June
I see a night full up with stars
        A ring adorns the moon.

And not one leaf from tree has fell
        And not one hair gone gray
I see it now just as it was
        The day I walked away.

A grand old barn, a farmer's pond,
        A great and sheltering tree,
The fishers seat, a large flat rock,
        The smaller boy is me.

The bobber sinks, the cane is bent
        The catch was youthful joy
I see it still, and there I am,
        A carefree, barefoot boy.

The Tuckahoe Sand Ridges

I'm betting not many of you will know anything at all about the Sand Ridges, or where they were, and were it not for Wayne Elkins, neither would I. I do know as a boy, thanks to Wayne, I spent many a happy hour wandering around those hills and hollows. That is what Wayne called the wilderness that lay between his home and Midway Road, especially the high ground that fronted on the west side of Elkins Road. His was the last house on the west side of Elkins Road before you reached Doane Lane. There was a lot of vacant hilly land behind his house and Midway Road.

It was there, about a quarter-mile off the road, that we built our clubhouse. It was rather small. Six boys would fit inside, if they all were standing up. But building it was where the fun was, not staying in it. Outside we had a pot-bellied stove with about four feet of stove pipe on it, and if the weather was cool we kept a fire going in it.

There were about six of us sitting around that stove one evening, probably telling jokes, when my brother A.B. got up and walked to the stove and opened its door. Then he reached into his pocket and pulled out a handful of 22 caliber rifle bullets, tossed them into the fire, closed the stove door and walked away. We all jumped up and tried to find something to get behind. Now a 22 cartridge in a rifle can send a lead bullet for a mile. Going off in a stove, it's not much more than a Chinese firecracker, but we didn't know that then. We heard them going off, sort of pop, pop, pop, and just like that, A.B. had created a memory.

Wayne was good at making things and once he constructed a teepee. It was well done. First, he covered it with insulating material, all kinds of stuff, like old blankets, quilts, and paper. Then he cut up some old linoleum and layered it on like overlapping roof shingles and made it waterproof. It was big enough for four or five guys to sleep in. Of course, we just had to do that, so we went there to spend the night. My buddy, C.H. Hardwick, came along. It was pitch dark outside, and we were all, or so I thought, inside the teepee laughing and talking.

Charles Weese was going to come later on, but perhaps only Wayne knew this. When he did come, he came quiet as a mouse, sneaking up to the back of the teepee. He found a place where he could put his arm under the outer edge, grabbed a leg, and tried to pull it out of the teepee, while making loud snorts and growls.

Inside the teepee, C.H. began to scream, while trying to free his leg. We didn't know what was wrong, but just about that time Charles let him go and rushed around to the entrance. He had created another memory.

Tuckahoe Snapshots

Not every memory is long enough for a story, and yet some are just too good to throw away. Thinking about this I thought I would group some into a sort of picture album, and call it snapshots, so the following is just that.

Robert Harp, "Baldy," coming down the hill by our house driving a hoodless 1936 Ford with Bruce King sitting on the front fender, pouring gas in the carburetor, to keep it running.

Wink Eye Brock on the stage at Smith School picking out Wild Wood Flower on his banjo with Hot Shot Elmer looking on.

Me, A.B., and Buddy Brock scouring the sage grass fields around Buddy's house (across from New Salem Church), searching for his little lost sister. Later his mother, Maurice, found her asleep under the bed.

Claude Smith hopping crazily around the big room at Smith School after he had somehow set off a book of matches in his pocket.

Boosie Smith, feeling no pain, unexpectedly, and after dark, dropping in at our house on Ridge Road, then sitting down at our piano, playing it, and singing us songs.

Daddy, O.C., driving his old Chevrolet panel truck to the River Breeze Drive-in Theater with the back end full of kids, and only paying for two.

C. H. while leaving the River Breeze (where we saw a scary movie), desperately trying to claw his way out of the back seat to escape the icy hand of death, after a cold drink behind him, tipped over and ran down his back.

Me, at about 5 years old, standing in our yard at the Smith School Road, Clifton Road intersection, watching the runaway horse and wagon of Howard and Cleo Cates thunder by; Howard leaning back on the reins, Cleo, pulling for dear life on the brakes. Howard told me many years later the horses ran away at Russell bridge and ran all the way home.

Henry Smith, nearing 70 years old, offering to race anyone from the store down to the creek bridge below Smith School and back. Nobody took the challenge.

Second-grade students sitting in a circle on the stage at Smith School with a little girl sitting next to the teacher, crying: a pool of water beneath her chair the teacher could not see. The teacher asking, what's wrong Honey? Me, wanting to help, but not quite knowing how.

Daddy, at the TVA & I Fair, helping me and A.B. to slip over the fence on McCalla Ave, behind the midway, to ride the rides.

The all-night, rise and fly Rook Games at our house on Slemp Road; the air full of cigarette smoke, and the smell of zippo lighter fluid. Never again have I played cards like that.

And last, me, falling asleep to the sound of rain falling on a tin roof.

Willie's Shoulder Bone
In Memory of Bill, Big Joe's Willie

It were not for lack of trying
Or from want'n, like as not
Cause if he turned his hand ta' work
Bill's best was what ya got.

Why...from plowin' fields to digg'n
Or ta cutt'n winter's wood
That Bill he always strived to do
The very best he could.

He wudn't big in stature, nor
was over blessed with looks
And none a'tall, from what I know'd
Was blessed at all in books.

But when it come to work'n, well,
It seems he had a mind
And to work'n hard at ever-thing
He really took a shine.

And honest too, a 'bout as much
As man's allowed to grow
And, as good a friend and neighbor as
A man will ever know.

So when ye take the measure of
How big a man ye be,
If ye come to Willie's shoulder bone
That's pretty big to me.

Veda Rocked Away

Not much of a house,
This house, as houses go
Just two small rooms
Heated by a fireplace, and an old wood kitchen stove
Set back about a hundred yards
From a narrow country road.

This house
Built of rough-hewn boards
And set on big flat stones
A humble dwelling is, but still it was a home
A good place to learn life's lessons
On humility and meekness.
And Veda is there
Alone in her rocker, before her dying fire.
Her rocker, this cold November day
Has rocked her little daily chores
And all her cares away.

The clock,
On the mantlepiece, gently ticks and tocks,
And softly chimes the hour
Wound faithfully this morning, as it always was before,
But the faithful hands that wound it up
Will wind it up no more.
The evening light slants through the window

and strikes the wooden floor
Laid by her husband's own two hands,
And made of rough wide boards,
Now smoothed and polished
By the mopping and the sweeping,
The cleaning dust and litter,
That accumulates and seems to go
With plain old simple living.

Her broom and mop
Are old like her,
Worn past the shape intended,
Will stay where they were put away
The time to mop and sweep has ended.
And all her simple tools,
The pots and pans she daily used,
Of what use now?
And of little worth, a bother left to throw away
By others, not by sisters or by brothers,
She has no longer any.

Her husband passed over long before,
But still at times, unthinking,
She would reach out for his hand to hold,
Or think perhaps she heard his steps
Upon the worn threshold

Now winter's cold surrounds the house,
Stands by the walls and windows,
And waiting there
For the fire's last flame to turn to dying embers
Will begin to creep through cracks in floors
And around the cracks in windows
And will be first
…To find her.

Television Comes to Tuckahoe

I don't remember the first time I learned there was such a thing as television, but the reality of it only came because Al Smith bought a set and had it in his house. His house stood next door to Smith Store, as most of you will know. He bought one in spite of the fact there were no TV stations in East Tennessee. Talk about an optimist.

Somehow a few of us wound up standing in Al's living room looking at his television set. It was turned on and was actually picking up a signal from Atlanta, Georgia. It was a baseball game being played in what looked like a bad snowstorm. That is the first memory I have of watching television, and I was not too impressed.

But the advantages of television, if we were to ever really get it, was not lost on anybody. It was one thing to go to a drive-in, or theatre, to watch a movie. But what if you could sit in your own home and watch one? That seemed almost too good to be true. Sometime later came the news that a television broadcasting station, WROL, was being built in Knoxville, TN.

In anticipation of what was soon to come, the Glenns, our next-door neighbors, bought a television set. On October 1, 1953, at 8 p.m. WROL was to start broadcasting. They were going to show a movie: "G.I. Joe."

It was a big event, an occasion to celebrate. I don't remember how it came about but on the date and time of that first broadcast, in the living room of the Glenns, there was standing room only.

Several of the younger ones present (including me) were seated on the floor in front of the TV. All the seating was full, some double occupied, and others were standing around the walls. There was an image on the screen of a test pattern, and we all had our eyes glued to that. It was a pattern with an Indian head, complete with headdress, circles, and numbers, and we got to know it real well.

They were scheduled to start broadcasting at 8 pm, but they didn't. Eight pm came and went, as did 9 pm, and 10 pm, and there was not a peep from the TV, but we were a patient lot, for nobody left. We had come to see history made, and it could happen at any second. Nobody was leaving.

Finally, about 11 pm, "G. I. Joe" showed up. It was as close to a miracle as we had ever seen. We were watching a movie in the living room! Despite the late hour, I think we all stayed and watched the entire film, and all headed home about 1 am.

Looking back, that whole episode seems comical, but at the time it did not seem so, not any more than going a great distance to see a solar eclipse would seem today. It was something we had never seen before. I don't regret the time. After all, you only get to do a first time, once.

Tuckahoe and the H. H. Smith General Store

I have been looking for something I wrote about H.H. Smith. Harry Henry Smith, the owner of H. H. Smith General Merchandise, our little Tuckahoe country store. When I got married and moved away from Tuckahoe it was still there, I was going to say still going strong, but looking back I doubt that it was. Henry and his wife, Mary, had both passed away by that time. Keeping the store going had passed to his son William, known to us all as simply, Boosie. Everybody loved Boosie, but Boosie's heart was not in storekeeping, it was in music. By that time most of the people in Tuckahoe had cars and were no longer tied to shopping at the local store: the times had changed. There was a price to pay for that progress for the tie that kept the community in close communion, if not broken, was being swept away with the changing times. When I moved back 10 years later it was gone. I'm glad Henry Smith was not around to see its demise.

I would say Henry was an extraordinary man, or at least in Tuckahoe, for he was an educated man. I remember right in the center of the store he had an office. He knew how to do accounting and there he kept a strict account of every item that was sold in the store in ledgers. Henry could write you out a deed, a bill of sale, or do your taxes.

Henry had been a bandleader and had run track when in school. I think he had a college education, as did at least one of his sons.

Henry's General store was the beating heart of the upper end of Tuckahoe. Probably half the people who visited that store, from day to day, did not go there to buy anything. There were always a few loafers hanging about, maybe playing checkers, or just passing time listening to the latest gossip. It was a place to go where you were welcome no matter your station in life, for there you would see folks you knew and could talk to about anything. In that way it was most like going to church is now, but you cannot just get up and go to church anytime you want, but you could to Henry's store.

Henry's house was just across the road from the store. I say was because the store is gone. Not a trace of the old store building remains, but the house is still there. Henry's grandson, Boosie's son, lives there now. If Mary could come back and see this present state I know exactly what she would say. "Lord a' mercy, Henry!… What in the world has happened?"

Virgin Moon

Long years may pass 'ere wisdom comes
To divine between the wise and dumb
- and so it was with me

For I thought once upon a time
My Father must have lost his mind
- to think the world was flat

How could he think the world was flat?
He went to school, and as for that
- he knew as much as me

I bare recovered from that shock
When he hit me with another rock
- this time about the moon

The moon to him seemed a holy thing
And man had not despite their claims
- ere set a foot upon it

A wide flat world - a virgin moon
Was my Pa crazy as a loon?
- I thought when I was young

But stranger still, it seemed to me
An air of calm tranquility
 - lingered round his door

And there it stayed, and when he died
I stood above his grave and cried
 - more than a man was gone

For if also passed too dark and doom
His flat earth with it's virgin moon
- it was hard for me to bear

If knowledge brought me ought but pain
In thinking round - where was the gain?
- Ah! take the sweet
        - and let the bitter go

Far better to dwell in a humble shack
'Neath a virgin moon, on a world that's flat
- than to have a troubled soul

Raab-ben-hoe

Where lived the creature Raab-ben-hoe
Exactly at I did not know
Or form he had or sound he made
From deep within the shadowed glades
I never saw nor heard.

But know I did, since two or three
While clinging to my Father's knee,
Where he revealed in whispers low
"Child, do avoid old Raab-ben-hoe,"
A lesson I remembered.

Who prowled the forest late at night,
who hated good, who shunned the light,
Who swept up foolish children and
Those caught are never seen again
Best to stay near our door.

But Father then would laugh a laugh
That made the scary feelings pass
Still, in the dark, safe in my bed,
I oft would cover up my head
Because of Raab-ben-hoe.

How dull a world this world I know
Would be without our Raab-ben-hoes'
Who brings us such delicious fright
So I warned my little ones tonight.
It was a father's duty.

With big bright eyes they hear, believe.
They know I never would deceive.
And then I laugh, I hold them tight,
They pound on me with great delight
Thanks to old Raab-ben-hoe.

1940s, A Day at Smith School

I keep going back and looking at the group picture of the students at Smith School, class of 1947. It almost has an unreal quality about it to me. Sort of like a dream I had and woke up from. A dream where you would like to go back to sleep and dream it again to fill in the details that are missing, but I can't do that. Still, I know some of you had the same dream, and can fill in parts, the names. and who lived where. But, alas. there are so few of us left who lived that dream, and when we are gone the living part of it will become as vapor and only the picture will remain.

Smith School had been around a very long time by the time I arrived there. I don't know what Smith School was like in the years gone by. I know it was there in 1895 and probably as a wood frame building because I saw it on a very old map.

The new brick building was built by the WPA. maybe in 1939. The building looked pretty nice to me. We had just moved back from Oak Ridge where I had started school, and was halfway through the second grade when I arrived. The school was divided by a moveable partition into two large rooms, which were called the "big room" and the "little room". The little room was actually bigger than the big room and referred to grade levels and not to size. Being only in the second grade I was placed in the "little room."

Standing in front of the school, that room would be on the right end on the school. I didn't much like being lumped together with first grade and third-grade students. At my former school, there was a feeling of competition among the students to achieve the best grades. I soon found out there was nothing like that going on at Smith School. That was left to the individual to desire or not. For most students, grades seemed to be something you just had to put up with.

Class of 1947

Funny, other than that impression, I remember very little about my time in the "little room" except that I had a crush on Mary Ann. Mary Ann soon left Smith School for Riverdale and broke my heart. Then, before I knew it, I graduat ed to the "big room". A whole new world. Howard Bailey, a man small in stature, was the teacher in the "big room". I was only in the fourth grade, but I stood as tall as Howard Bailey. Most of the boys in the sixth grade. and some in the fifth grade, literally towered over him. Mr. Bailey had a hard task to keep some kind of control over that rather rowdy bunch. He resorted to methods of discipline to do this that would get a teacher fired today...if not jailed.

One method was to put a small circle on the blackboard just high enough to make you stand on tiptoe to put your nose inside the circle. If your nose dropped out of the circle a swift whack with a paddle got it back in the proper place.

In the front of the school. where the entry doors were, the only windows were over the doors and in the cloakrooms. The back of the school in contrast was all windows from five foot up. I remember sitting there in September and looking out at the blue sky through the green tree leaves and wanting so bad to be out there instead of sitting at a school desk.

There was no plumbing in the school at all. No bathroom and no running water. There was a well pump outside connected to a long pipe with holes in it that water would shoot upward from... as long as some strong boy operated the hand pump. This way several kids could get a drink at one time. It was good water, and after the school closed,

New Salem Church put an electric pump in the well, built a well house, and supplied water to the church. I don't know if they still use that or not.

There were two outhouses (girls and boys) placed far apart in the woods behind the school. They were not places to linger long in. It was just good to have a private place to do your business. But we all had them at home so we were all used to that. It was just the way it was back then.

When I first went to Smith School, in the winter they heated each room with a big potbelly stove. The school had a basement where a supply of coal was stored. Maybe some boy from the "big room" started the fires and fed them during the day, but they also needed to be cleaned out and the ashes removed and disposed of. Makes me wonder if they were paid anything to do that? Soon after I started school there, a coal furnace was installed. Whoo Hoo!, and the potbelly stove years were over at Smith School. But not at home, and to be truthful there was something cozy about hugging up near a warm stove on a cold winter day.

We all walked to school, and most kids used shortcuts to get there. By road, it might be two miles or more to school.

But cutting through the woods or over the fields could cut that in half. It wasn't possible for everyone to do that, but those who could did. Smith School was in Knox County, but quite a few students came from Sevier County and nobody seemed to care.

Stop and look again at the picture. Do you see anything different about it? Take notice there are no overweight kids. There were some rather skinny, but not for lack of food.

It really wasn't much of an education but it taught kids to read and write, do simple math, and not much else that would be of much use in later life. But I can truthfully say I enjoyed my years there and made a bunch of life-long friends.

Hog Killing Day in Tuckahoe

It's a little dim in memory now. Like an old photograph that has faded out around the edges, but the center, though clouded, still brings to mind what is now lost in time. Maybe I was around seven years old, and we had just moved back to the home place from Oak Ridge, and it must have been in the springtime when Daddy came home with two cute spotted baby pigs. He had built a pen for them away from the house up by the woods, and that is where he put them.

"These are not pets" he said, "so don't fool around this pen getting friendly with them, and don't give them names. Just don't fool around this pen at all", and so we didn't.

One little item I have not seen mentioned in any google search on hog killing. Maybe it's not politically correct to talk about castration, but nobody raised a male pig for the purpose of eating it without having this little item taken care of. Bill, or Big Joe's Willie, as he was also known, usually took care of that duty for Daddy.

And so, all spring and summer, and into the fall, the pigs kept growing and putting on weight. They had a steady diet of leavings from the garden mixed with store-bought hog feed and water, which we called slop. Daddy also pulled these big roadside plants he called hogweeds and fed them to the pigs, and the pigs loved them. I was always amazed at all the stuff Dad knew how to do.

Hog killing time arrived with the cold weather. You needed a cold snap of several days when the temperature was going to stay at about the temp inside a modern refrigerator. This usually happened in mid to late November.

If you planned on killing, dressing out, and working up the meat on two 500 lb. hogs you are going to need help. Frank Hancock's boys would come and help daddy. The Hancock boys, Paul, Adam, and one more, whose name will not come to mind, were not boys, but big strong men. They brought the rifle to kill the pigs with. One shot right between eyes usually did the trick, but I remember one time it didn't. I remember that one hog that wouldn't die. It was a very big white hog. They shot it, but instead of falling over it took off running and squealing. In anticipation of dragging the dead hog to the scalding vat, they had torn down a portion of the hog pen fence, and so the pig got out. They had to run it down and tackle it. Two of them sat on it and the other one shot it, again and again. Seven times they shot that hog before they did him in. Later we found out why: the skull of that hog was over an inch thick. Then came the bloody part. Sticking the hog with a large knife and letting all its blood run out on the ground. After that was done, there really wasn't much blood at all in the rest of the work.

But getting back to the hog kill'n routine, it was; kill the hogs, scald them in a big vat of water with a fire under it, and remove all their hair; then hang them up, head down, (which was not an easy thing to do), remove their entrails into a big tub, and cut off their heads. What was left hanging up would then be split down the middle and divided into two halves. This was taken into the smokehouse (which we never smoked anything in), and there my dad worked without stopping. First, he had to divide the hogs into hams, shoulders, and middlens. Next, he would trim off the parts of the meat that would turn into sausage and lard. Then he had to salt down the trimmed parts to preserve them. The goal was to preserve, in one form or another, all that was edible, or useful, in those pigs, and almost everything was. There was fat, bacon, hams, shoulders, middlens, tenderloin, ribs, liver, sausage, backbone, chitlins,(no, take that one back, we didn't do chitlins), cracklings, pigs feet, hog jowl, souse meat, the list went on and on. The old saying "you can eat it all but the squeal" is mostly true.

While Daddy worked in the smokehouse we worked in the kitchen grinding sausage. Daddy would bring in the meat for us to grind. It took hours of turning that crank. Mama would be seasoning the sausage, frying it up, and putting it into jars for canning. After she had a full jar she would pour hot grease from the frying pan into the jar, seal it with a lid, and turn it upside down. The grease formed a seal that bacteria could not get through. While this was going on she would also be rendering out the fat outside in a big iron kettle, turning it into lard. It's hard to remember now just how long all that took, but I am thinking two long hard days.

So between all of us working hard together, we turned those pigs into a store of supplies that would help take us through the winter, spring, and summer, until it was hog killing time again.

I must have gone through that family tradition at least 12 times, but at 19, I got married, and left my old home behind. I didn't miss hog killing, but I suppose they missed me being there and helping them with the work. I am sorry to say I never gave that much thought until right now while writing this. But shortly after I got married we moved to Florida and I guess my mind became occupied with life in a different world. I can't say it was better, only different.

Sitting here writing this, I remember Mama frying up a batch of fresh tenderloin. To this day one of the best things I have ever eaten.

Tales from Tuckahoe

Turning on the Light

Shadows lurked in all the corners
From the fireplace flickering light
As we hugged the hearth for warmth
On a cold December night.

And from fireplace to the kitchen
Stood one oil lamp in between
With not much illumination
From the glow of kerosene.

Both the time and place were different
From the days that were ahead
For with dark, just like the chickens,
We would hurry off to bed.

But one day stands out in memory
From the time I left the womb
Was the night we drove the shadows
From the corners of the room.

From a glass globe on the ceiling
Came a little piece of sun
With a power in its shining
Which had only just begun.

No other wonder I remember
Though each brought their own delight
Compare at all nor measure up
To turning on the light.

Whittling

A word or two on whittling here
        That mindless loafer's trade
A task best done, if done at all,
        Reclining in the shade.

A messy job, as slender shaves
        Fall round the whittlers seat,
And cedar coils, like tiny springs,
        Adorn the whittlers feet.

The whittler carves no work of art
        For other folk to see.
As stick bent, he is content
        With what will be will be.

It is a craft that's valued most
        Among the whittling crew,
And was a time, a while ago,
        I use to do it to.

Where I was taught a lesson 'bout
        How metal made the knife,
And how that is related to
        The broader facts of life.

For whittling knifes do not attain
    heir razor edge alone,
The dull they were it must be left
    upon the whittler's stone.

The Marble King of Smith School
A small tragedy

"For everything, there is a season." And for boys, there were seasons for things at Smith School. A season for yo-yos, a season for rolling old tires, and a season for playing marbles, and we played marbles for keeps…serious stuff.

This was a long time ago and we didn't have costly toys, but that has never stopped kids from playing. Seems kind of crazy now, even to me, to think of making a toy out of an old worn-out tire, but you could roll it, and it would go where you pushed it, and it wasn't so hard to imagine you were driving a car…Varommmm!

But marbles were different because it was competitive and required one to develop a bit of skill to be good at it. No imagination was required.

At first, I lost a lot of marbles, and that made me sort of analyze what I was doing wrong. One thing I saw was that it was really hard to shoot a marble along the ground and make it go straight. Any little gravel or lump it happened to hit could divert it from the target, Hmmmm…? What if you could shoot it hard enough that it never had to touch the ground until it hit the target? Well to make a long story short, that was the method I worked on. That required using a different technique than anyone else was using, but eventually, I got good at it, so much so that I started winning a lot of marbles.

I thought it would not be long before others would see what I was doing and copy it, but that never happened. And before long I had won all the marbles, and the fun went out of it for me, and for everybody else. So I retired as the Marble King of Smith School, with a whole sewing machine drawer full of marbles.

It was almost Christmas and my Sunday school class at New Salem Baptist Church had drawn names. You know how that works, the person whose name you drew, you bought a present for. I was excited about that…just thinking I would get a present.

Christmas came, and we were at church, and Santa Claus was there giving out the presents. Finally, he called my name and I rushed to get my present and hurried back to my seat. It was a small box, but that was ok. I will never forget what happened next. I sat down and took the wrapping paper off the box, broke a bit of tape, and opened it… and there I found…a small bag of…marbles. Maybe for any other kid, it would have been fine. And not long before that, it would have been true for me but if there was one thing in all the world the Marble King did not want, or need, it was more marbles. But maybe I got just what I deserved.

Here then is a lesson in human nature. Here is the how and why fortunes are made and hoarded away in vaults where it does nobody any good. What good were those marbles doing me, or anybody, stored away in a drawer? I should have taken them back to school and given them all back to the other kids. That it never occurred to me to do that, speaks volumes about how being selfish just comes natural to us.

Sometime later Dad had a well dug right beside our house. Soon there would be no more carrying water from the spring. He was going to put in a hand pump. That meant he would have to build a platform to anchor the pump on, with room enough to stand beside the pump.

He poured it out of concrete. I looked at that small wet concrete slab and had an idea. I went into the house and got my marbles, and I imbedded that day, month, and year, in marbles in that wet concrete. Our old house is gone now, as is the hand pump. But I think the marbles are still there as my memorial to the Marble King, out of the sunlight now, enclosed in an old well house, and out of sight. All the rest were lost in time.

A Day at the Movies, Somewhere around 1950

My buddy C. H. and I came into some money, maybe by hauling hay or working in tobacco. Two days of that would have netted us about $6.00 each. Saturday was coming up and we thought we would go to Knoxville and go to the movies as a treat. By this time, we had reached the age we could go by ourselves. So early Saturday morning found us seated on the bus, headed to Knoxville, and the movies.

The problem was we got to town at an early hour and most of the theaters were not open. Our bus had put us out near Market Square and walking through it we saw the Crystal Theater was open, and so for 10 cents apiece we turned in there. Think of it… A serial, a newscast, a cartoon, and a movie, and all for a dime. How could you pass that up? I don't know now if the rest of the day was actually planned or not, so all I can tell you is how it turned out.

When we came out of the Crystal we headed on down Market Street to the end of the block and turned for Gay Street…and there was the Roxie, now open, and we thought, what the heck, and we went in for 25 cents each. Double Feature? Maybe.

When we got out it must have been near noon and we were a bit hungry so we looked up a Krystal diner and bought some hamburgers at 10 cents each.

We walked on down Gay Street to the Riviera Theater. Now we were moving up in the world to a better class of theater, and movie, so the ticket prices kept going up... maybe a little less than 50 cents each, as I remember.

Later, when we came out, without a second thought, we headed for that grand movie palace that was, and still is, the Tennessee Theater. What a place! The long marble-floored lobby; the hanging chandeliers, the carpeted stairs that led up to the balcony; we even thought the men's restroom was ritzy. But the balcony was where we wanted to go, so up we went and seated ourselves down on the very first row where there was nothing between us, and the movie screen...but air.

I don't remember the name of any of the movies we saw, but that doesn't matter because no matter what they were we would have gone in and watched them. The proof is that after we came out of the Tennessee Theater, we still had time to spare before we could catch our bus home, so, naturally, we headed on down Gay Street to the Bijou for one more round.

But it was one round too many, for our eyes were beginning to hurt, and after only a few minutes we had to leave for we could not tolerate the glare of the movie screen anymore.

The above is not a thing anybody would do today. But then, movies were a treat that could only be enjoyed at a movie theater, or at a drive-in movie. Then, it was something we thought we couldn't get enough of. Turned out… we were wrong. Our eyes soon returned to normal, but we had done something, maybe a little crazy, we would never forget. However, it does bring a ring of truth to the old bromide, "a fool and his money are soon parted".

\

A Memory of Peaches

On Dale Ave, just across the street from Witt Lumber Company, there once stood a large tobacco warehouse. In the summer, along about July, it would be filled with truckloads of peaches from South Carolina and Georgia. Every summer at that time Dad would go there to buy peaches for canning and most of the time I went along. He would usually buy two bushels of peaches, but it was not a hasty process by any means. It really mattered to him to get the right kind of peaches, so Dad took his time about picking them out.

Dad would only buy Alberta or Hale peaches. So he walked among the trucks asking questions until he found the right truck. Then he would eat one of the peaches to test the taste. He wanted a peach that was sweet but tangy, and if it passed the test, off we went back home with two (maybe three) bushels of peaches.

Alberta and Hale's peaches are really fuzzy peaches and before you could can them you had to peel them. Dad would get out the big washtub, fill it with water and pour in the peaches. You could not peel those peaches without doing that first because that fuzz would eat you up if you didn't. It took a long time to peal two bushels of peaches because you needed to make the peeling as thin as you could to avoid throwing away much of the peach itself. But even so, the peelings were not wasted: we fed them to the pigs.

If you ran across an over-ripe peach, or a badly bruised one, you put them off to the side without peeling them. After all the good peaches were canned Mama would take the rejects and make peach butter out of them. There is no better type of jelly than peach butter made with the right kind of peaches. But if you are going to enter a jar for judging at the fair you had better put some lemon juice in it to lighten up the color. Not knowing that cost me a blue ribbon once.

Before you were done with pealing peaches your fingers would get all white and wrinkled up. It must have been from more than just having your hands wet with water for a long time. I think handling all those peaches helped cause that.

Anyway, after all that work we had peach pies, and fried pies filled with peach butter, all winter long, and sometimes just a jar of peaches.

As Good as It Gets

Now winter just comes.
    But there was a time
When you had to prepare for it,
    When you had to get ready
Or freeze, or starve.

But, if you had done your homework,
    Chopped all the wood,
Filled the pantry with canned goods
    From the garden,
Filled the smokehouse
    With cured ham and bacon,
Laid up potatoes and apples in the root cellar,
    Topped out the crib with corn
And stuffed the barn with sweet smelling hay,
    Then you were ready,
Let winter come and do its worst.

Then the crisp days of autumn,
    With its deep blue skies
White clouds and trees decked out in
    Joseph's coats, brought a
Feeling of satisfaction, well being
    And thankfulness
Words are powerless to express.

And if you were there
>Warm before your hearth
Bathed in the bounty of the land
>Wrapped in the goodness of God
Paid by the rewards of honest toil
>And surrounded by family and love
You felt in your heart,
>At least for an hour or two,
It was about as good as earthly life
>Was ever going to get.

And I suppose an hour or so
>Of feeling like that
Is about all the mortal heart
>Can stand.

Smith School and the Columbus Stockade Blues

Had there been no Smith School, this memory would not exist, because the event it records would never have happened. Smith School was the only place in Tuckahoe where a large gathering of people could assemble that was not religious in nature. It is a good example of the mysterious role the work of fate has over events, and how that can change how our life may turn out. There are several such forces at work in this story. I will leave it to the reader to ponder on this if they have a mind to.

I don't know what Smith School was like in the years before my time, but when I was there, it was a solid red brick building with a basement where coal was stored to heat the building in winter. Each room had a potbelly stove which some of the bigger boys fed with coal in winter. The brick building was built by the WPA, a public works program brought about by the Great Depression.

They used the school as a place to sign up for ration stamps during WWII. Sometimes children would get vaccinations there, too. Once, when I was small, Mama took me there to get a vaccination and to get ration stamps for sugar at the same time. She told me I would get my vaccination first and then we would go in the next room to get her sugar stamps. When we left I wasn't happy and I told her I was never going to get shots for sugar again.

But the school did have a stage and that made it a good place for public or community gatherings, and for entertainment purposes, such as movies, programs by musical groups, even cakewalks or pie suppers.

By the time of my story, a cafeteria and restrooms had been added to the school. That cafeteria was where the event told here took place.

My best friend at the time the story takes place was Don Lane. We hung around together quite a bit, and Don could drive, and usually had a car or access to one, so we rode around together to one place or the other. Don loved to sing and was good at it, and I wasn't all that bad, so we would be going down the road singing some song we both knew, but there wasn't really very many of those, but there was one we both knew, "The Columbus Stockade Blues."

This would have been nothing if Don had not been able to sing harmony, but he could, and I had no idea how to do that, and because he could, it made the songs sound pretty good to us, and apparently to a few others also.

Cas Walker was going to bring his local TV show "The Farm and Home Hour" performers to Smith School for a show. Plus there would be a talent contest and the winner would be invited to perform on the Farm and Home Hour. I don't think Don and I knew about that part when we decided to drop in and watch the show.

When the talent contest part of the show started, a few people in the audience had heard Don and I sing and started urging us to get up and sing a song, and sort of pushed us into doing it, and so we did, and what else could we sing, but "The Columbus Stockade Blues." Was there any competition? All that happened over 60 years ago, so I really don't remember, only that we won the right to appear on the "Farm and Home Hour". I don't think we ever seriously considered doing that, so we might have deprived the world, (or spared it of), The Tuckahoe Two, and the "Columbus Stockade Blues."

Noble

Serenely noble he, rangy, rock-ribbed, redbone hound.
He wasn't mine
But we used to hunt together time to time
From the gravel road going past his master's house,
I'd stand and shout,
And if he was home here'd come old Noble out.

He'd wag his tail and I'd squat down
and scratch his head a time or two,
Was our little way of saying Howdy-Do!
Old Noble hound, he was a first-grade
possum dog no doubt!
Hunt'n possums was all he knowed,
and all he cared about.

Yeller moon be rising, with one old
smoked up lantern for a light
Hunting possums is a job you did at night.
Then, off we'd go, he'd take the lead,
Old Noble never followed me,
That's the way it was, and the way it had to be.

High Ridge or hollow, bugle mouth dog baying, resonat'ng
In the dark, told if he was trailing or was tree'n by his bark.
Noble, he'd be wait'n, holding faithful, 'neath his tree,
Have a possum grinning down on him and me.

Our hunt'n done, he'd turn and look at me,
Then he was gone,
I had to fetch him out but I never took him home.
Just fondly recollect'ng
One deep throated, barrel-chested hound, he wasn't mine,
But we used to hunt together time to time.

Fox and Hound

When Henry was the swift red fox
And I the chasing hound
His part was to hide in among the trees
And mine to hunt him down.

And as the wind on a bright spring day
Whips through a cloudless sky
Through the oak and the pine and the alder bush
 So Henry ran and I.

And many the tangled way he led
And many the hills he climbed
And many the brook he waded through
With me real close behind.

But he got me lost out in those woods
In the forest dark and deep
And the only prayer I knew, I prayed
The lord my soul to keep.

For I'd wandered in a bit too far
With no path - that I could see
So I had to yell for that durn fox
To come and rescue me.

As was Henry's way he saved my face
For he sailed at me some stones
And when I saw him tearing through the woods
I chased that rascal home.

And so, Henry, he was my hero.
There, I said it without shame
And amid the graves of the valiant dead
Is a cross with Henry's name.

And I missed him…still I miss him
For his passing left me marked
And I can't help but think about him
When I'm walking in the dark.

And on starry nights, should I hear a hound
It takes me back in time
To when I was a hound who loved to run
And the fox was a friend of mine.

On Going to Town from Tuckahoe

There was a time, about seventy years ago, when going to Knoxville from Tuckahoe was quite an experience. For one thing, hardly anybody owned a car, so if you wanted to go to town you had no choice but to ride the bus. Lewis Bus Lines provided the transportation.

They ran a bus early in the morning to town, and a bus to return from town late in the afternoon. There was no other choice, so if you were going it would be an all-day affair, like it or not.

It was a long trip and not a straight shot as it is today by interstate highway. The bus took a tortuous route and picked up passengers all along the way. The bus route went by way of Thorngrove Pike to Asbury, then by Strawberry Plains Pike, across Boyd's Bridge to River Side Drive, and on into Knoxville. All told about 25 miles and the trip took well over an hour. So you did not do it unless you were going to work, or had some shopping to do for things you had to have and could not purchase at the local general store.

Shopping centers were far in the future, and that meant that everyone in all directions who had shopping to do, went to Knoxville to do it, and Knoxville, especially on a Saturday, was a busy place. The sidewalks were jammed with people. The streets were filled with buses, electric trolley cars, and not a few cars. Most of the foot traffic was either on Gay Street, or one block over on Market Square. If you were pinching pennies, you shopped on Market Square.

Before I finish let me say a bit about the Gay Street Terminal Building, which was a bus station, and one of my favorite places in Knoxville. When I went to town with my Mom, when she got tired, we would go to that bus station to rest for there were plenty of benches there. When you walked into the bus station you did not see any buses, just benches, for the buses came into the station by underground routes. There were stairs to get down to the gates where the buses loaded and unloaded. An announcer would tell over the PA system where a bus was loading and all the places that bus was going. If you were bound for another town, like Maryville, this was the place to catch that bus. I only caught a bus out of that station once, and that was to go to Maryville where my Grandparents lived. I thought I was really living it up.

But the biggest reason I liked it was because I could buy comic books there. There was a pole stand there which had comics books in racks all around it. Mom would give me a dollar and with that I could buy 10 comic books. I cannot tell you how much joy that brought me. I guarded them with my life, and when I got home with them I read them over and over again, then added them to my stash.

Sometimes I traded them with Fuzzy Russell who liked western comics. I only bought Disney, or Looney Tunes comics, so we each would wind up with comics we never would have bought ourselves.

Of Elkins Road, and Wooden Wagons

I found, online, an old 1895 map of the 22nd District of Knox County, TN, (where Tuckahoe is located). The map not only shows roads and landmarks but the names of people who lived on those roads. Most names you would recognize as families who still live here today. There was a Smith School on Smith School road even then. Elkins Road was there, but it didn't loop all the way back to Smith School Road in 1895. It ended at the home of a man named Joe Elkins. Joe was the only person shown who lived on that road in 1895. Almost all the roads in Tuckahoe are named after people, or families, who lived on that road and may have been, like Joe, the very first one who did.

About halfway around Elkins Road, I remember there was a small, and very old, log house set far back from the road in a grown-up field: Maybe it was Joe's, for it was a long-abandoned structure. It was said that the door of that house would not remain closed, even if you closed it securely. That later, when you came by, it would be open again. Whether that was true or not I cannot say for I never went near it.

Elkins Road, for its length, might have been the most heavily populated road, per mile, in Tuckahoe. When I try to recall the families who lived on that road when I was a boy,

I think of Clifton 2, Elkins 2, Stinnett 1, Brock 3, Smith 2, Weese 1, Glenn 3, Brown 1, Cody 1, Pitts 1, Hancock 1, Maples 1, King 1, and Wells. Maybe you can think of more or put first names to some of these. Do you remember a Hot Shot Glenn, who would start all he would say with, "Shoot Um"?

Elkins Road was not a road you would use to go anywhere except to a place on Elkins Road, and I had not a reason to drive on that road for a very long time. But I did drive around it while I was writing this. I was surprised to see how it had changed. All the houses where my friends had lived were gone. In fact, only one house was left of all those I remembered. The old green log house where Bob Clifton lived is still standing.

As a boy, if going to Elkins Road, I would walk to Smith Store first. Just to the left of the store, there was a gate to a field and beyond it was the remnant of an old dirt road. That road led across the field to the woods behind New Salem Church; from there a footpath led through the woods and came out on Elkins road. Since hardly anyone owned a car back then, the path was well used to get to the store, the school, or the church, from Elkins Road.

In those days, there were three dead-end roads that led off Elkins road. The road that led to Hollis Glen's house, the road that Frank Hancock and Coot Clifton lived on, and Doane Lane where I think some Smith families lived. There are more of those roads or driveways now.

I had gone to Elkins Road one day to see Wayne, a friend of mine, to see what he was up to, for he was always up to something. He and I, and Charles, were standing near the woods behind Charles' house. We were looking down a long steep cleared path that led down to the hollow. There was a sharp left-right curve halfway down. At our feet sat the reason for the cleared path: a wooden wagon. I heard Wayne had built a wooden wagon, and I had gone over to see it. It really looked cool, even had a large hubcap steering wheel that controlled ropes attached to each end of the front axle. I call it a wooden wagon because it was all made of wood, the wheels, the axles, the frame; the only metal in it were the bolts and nails that held it together. I rode it two or three times down the hill, and never made it all the way down: I kept sliding off the wagon seat going around the curve. But the hard part was pulling it back up the hill. It was really heavy.

Later on, I built my own version of a wooden wagon. Mine was a brazen copy of Wayne's. I had learned nothing of value riding his except what it looked like. It took me two days or more to build it. When it was as finished, as it was ever going to get, I wanted to try it out. I pulled it back deep into the woods, searched out a good place for a road, and cleared one down a steep hill. I pulled my wagon up to the top of the hill (not easy) and rode it to the bottom. I didn't have the strength left, nor the inclination to do it again. I stood there and looked up to the top of the hill, and down at my new creation, and knew in my heart there wasn't enough fun in it to pull it up the hill again. I realized that without friends to share the toil and the joy it was no good, and my friends already had one; so I just walked away, just left it setting there, leaving it to nature to dispose of. Might have been easier if I had not built it mostly of green hickory.

FOOTNOTE: Many years later, I chanced to go by the place where I had left that wagon. There was not a trace of it to be seen…nothing! It was in a deep hollow prone to flooding after heavy rains. Time, rot, and rushing water had removed, or covered, all trace of my wagon. Nothing was left of that fruitless adventure…unless…you counted me.

Is That You?

Ah, Henry, I tire at last of length of days
This part you never knew
For the summer sun shines not as bright
And not so many stars at night.
As in those days we used to play
Way back when we were young.

And yesterday I slipped away and walked
Down to the creek
The place we used to fish and swim
And I had a thought of jump'n in
But I'm way too old
And it was cold
And I could hear you laughing.

It has not changed that much, you know,
Not near as much as me,
For still the channeled water flows
And still, it burbles as it goes
Into the bowl
Of the swimming hole
Long time I stood and listened.

The green fields lay with new-mown hay
And smelled to me as sweet
But the old foot log has long since gone
We used to cross on our way home.
It's gone the way
Of our boyish play
And I've grown too proud to wade.

So how does the land lay, Henry!
The land, the place you are?
For here my time is nearly spent
Soon I shall follow where you went.
Sometimes I dream
We'll find a stream
Well, you know how we are.

I don't know why I thought of you
Or why I'm taking so,
Why sixty years at least have passed
Since we ran in that new-mown grass.
I used to follow ore hill and hollow
But such running days are past.

But Henry, while I have your ear
And if it ain't no trouble
I thought I'd ask you strike a light,
You know, how I was scared at night.
And lately when the dark is fall'n
I seem to hear this voice a' calling
It seems to be a' calling me.
Henry!   Is that you?

John McFine

John McFine was a farmer's son.
Big green valley was his home.
But another smaller valley lay
Cross the mountain from his own.

A smith in that other valley
Shoed the horses of McFine.
John's father said his favorite mare
Was needing shoes this time.

He said, John halter up the mare
And take her to the smith,
And tell the man to take his time
As they got to last a bit.

John's mother packed him up a lunch
And he was on his way,
And little dreamed the tragic doom
Awaiting him that day.

He soon crossed ore the mountain
Down to the valley floor
And the road on which he traveled
It passed the parson's door.

L. Clayton Cate

With the parson's youngest daughter
Washing clothes beneath a tree,
To John McFine the prettiest thing
He thought he'd ever see.

And where once walked a carefree lad
The carefree John McFine,
From that time on he couldn't get
Her image off his mind.

Oh well, he got the mare all shod.
Oh well, he went back home.
But the John McFine returning
Was not the John who'd gone.

Do You Remember the Tuckahoe Dips?

The dips on Smith School Road were
Best crossed going a little too fast
With a passenger new to Tuckahoe
Not expecting the bottom would fall out
And the road would rise up to meet them
And that both would happen
In very quick succession
But, you can't do that anymore.

Or when going the other way
You could actually defy gravity
Be launched up into the air
Until the top of your head hit the roof
Stopping your ascent up short.
Of course, then both you and the car
Had to come back down to earth.
Thud!! But all that is gone now.

Interstate 40 came and leveled out the dips.
Now you can traverse the same spot
Going west, at over seventy miles per hour
And be bored to death
You gain a little, you lose a little,
The price of smoothing things out
Is higher for some than for others.
Progress is what we call it.

Soon the memory of the Dips
Will pass away too.
Which is true for many things
The older folk know the younger
Generations have no idea of
And won't, unless someone writes it down.
My wife says I want everyone to know what I know
Which helps explain why I like to write.

P.S. Some will know, but some may wonder, just where the dips were on Smith School Road. They were located just about halfway between the intersection of Smith School Road with Thorne Grove Pike, and Hayes Hill, which is the hill Rod Stinnett lived on. I think the westbound lanes of I-40 took them out.

Moving Day by Horse and Wagon, 1943

The Will and Sis Clifton house on Clifton Road has long been empty, but is still standing, and looks pretty sound for its age. With a little work, it could still be livable. It must have been a well-built house. I knew Will and Sis pretty well, since at times they would babysit for my Mom if she had business in town. One of those times stands out clearly in my mind. I remember eating with them. They had those blue and white China plates with nature scenes on them. You can still buy those plates, for I have seen them in stores.

For that meal, Sis was serving white soup beans and she had biscuits for bread. It was a good meal. Mr. Clifton was eating with us. I remember he was drinking coffee, and he was dunking his biscuit in his coffee. That looked good to me and I wanted to try it. He said, "You won't like it." But he let me try it, and he was right. I thought it was awful. But to this day I cannot see one of those blue and white plates without thinking of white soup beans.

Those days, so very early in my life, are hard to put dates to. At the time of this story, we lived at the intersection of Smith School Road and Clifton Road, in an old frame house that belonged to Humphrey Smith, who was a brother of Henry Smith. Humphrey had married my Dad's sister, Rossi.

But we did not live there much longer for dad bought some land on Slemp Road that had a house on it and we moved there. I remember we were moved by horses and wagon, and it well could have been the horses and wagon of Will Clifton. My only memory of that day is sitting in the wagon as we moved away and looking back at the home we were leaving. I think it was a sad day for me, for I liked that place and didn't like the new house much at all.

In trying to put a time frame to all this I remember I started school in Oak Ridge which would have made me 6 years old, and about 1944. So the move in the wagon may have been 1943. Wow, that makes me feel old. Bet not many are alive who can remember moving by horse and wagon.

So I must have been 4 to 5 years old when the above dinner happened that I remember so well. Sis was seated to my left and Mr. Clifton was seated to my right. I can still see it in my mind. Isn't it strange what your mind chooses to remember? I read somewhere that you only remember the things that were really good, or really bad. Those must have been really good white soup beans.

Will Clifton was a true farmer who made his living off the land. He had barns, cows, and horses. (I, at one time, knew the names of his horses). He had one barn near his house and I remember wheat being threshed there. I remember A.B. and I sneaking in that barn, getting a leaf of curing tobacco, and taking it home to chew on…then getting sick on it, turning green, and throwing up.

By that time of this story, Will and Sis's children had grown up, married, and moved out, so to me, Will and Sis seemed old people, but still able to carry on with life as they always had. I know some of his grandchildren had gone off to fight in the Great War.

Will Clifton had to travel about a mile to get to his creek bottom farm. To get there he traveled over what is now Ridge Road, which is mostly in Sevier County. It was a rough ridge top road Sevier County did not claim, and it did not then, nor even now, have a right of way. So Will was one of the few people concerned with keeping the road passable. He did this by hauling rocks in his wagon and filling in the mud holes on his way home. But though it was a rough road it was not so bad for horse and wagon, and unlike now, he would not have been bothered by automobiles.

Cooperation

I know something of cooperation
For I have put my hands to a cross cut saw,
When in the fall, my Father and I
Walked to that pile of limbless trees.
And I on one end and he on the other,
Let the saw glide, effortless and smooth,
Slowly gently to set a groove;
Then, almost like a dance the crosscut fled
Back and forth and also sang,
And deeper, deeper into the wood.
He would push and I would pull.
The saw seeming not to pause nor stop.
It's tempered steel, our perspiration
And one by one the wood pile dropped.
I know something of cooperation.

Youth's Wages

l remember growing up
And living in the country
When I was big enough to work.
All day a' hauling hay
We'd bust a gut tossing round
Bales as big as we were.
And three dollars was the wages
For a long eight-hour day.

Then home and take a quickie bath
In a pan of water,
Removing all the dust and dirt
Someone was gonna see.
Some faded pants an ironed shirt
And we were fit for travel,
For all that hard-earned money
Was just bust'n out our jeans.

Pack a herd of boys in
A forty-seven Chevy,
Dividing up the cost of gas,
So we could have a ride.
Then we were smoking down the road
Headed for the city
Rolling with a buddy
Who had barely learned to drive.

At the city park
Throwing balls at metal bottles,
Win a kewpie doll,
Or some other useless thing.
Ride the tilt-a-whirl and
Throw up on somebody.
Or go around in circles
At the roller skating rink.

Wink at all the pretty girls
Skating in short dresses.
If they smiled back at you
You turned red as berry pie.
At twelve o'clock, we headed home
With everybody busted.
We wasted all our money
But we really had a time.

Looking back on those old days
It was kinda tame and silly
Compared to all the stuff
The young folks can do today.
But we were young and our world was young
And the future bright and cheery
With the worries of tomorrow
All a million miles away.

Emily Fair

Isn't that a pretty name? It's the name of a lady who lived in Tuckahoe perhaps a century ago. The date is uncertain. Because I only learned of her through conversations I had with my neighbor Charles, known to most who knew him, and to me, as J.B.

J.B. was a veteran of the Second World War. He was there from the invasion of Normandy until the war was over. When his captain found out how old he was (16) he was assigned to drive an army truck. That may have saved his life. He drove it off a landing craft onto the Normandy beach, and later all over Europe until the war was over. He was only 19 when he came home from the war. He lived in the house just across the road from mine.

He was an interesting man to talk to; was a big fan of baseball; played the guitar and could sing really well. We were good friends. I really miss that man since he passed away.

He told me what life was like in Tuckahoe when he was young. He told me that the folks were not as friendly then as they are now. He told me about Emily Fair.

Emily Fair was known, according to J.B., as one who gleaned cornfields and garden plots after the harvest to find what had been overlooked, or thought not worth picking up. She was sort of doing what Ruth in the Bible did. He said one might run upon a small pile of corn cobs on top of a wooded ridge where Emily had stopped and shelled out what treasure she had found.

He said he had literally run into her once on a dark night on a creek bottom wagon road. He said she grunted, told him to watch where he was going, and walked on.

I think she roamed the hills and hollows of Tuckahoe mostly at night, and mostly unseen, and became a sort of local legend.

I doubt I would have brought this up had her name been Sadie Johnson, (no offense intended Sadie), but the name Emily Fair was just too poetic to let her drop into the realm of forgotten lore.

And so I told you

Burnt Oil

I appreciate that some of you like the stories that I write, and maybe especially those I write about Tuckahoe, and what it was like when I was growing up here. No story is very long and drawn out because nothing I remember was. They are snippets of things that happened. If they seem to be longer, it's because I add in descriptions and details to make the story come alive as well as I can. Otherwise, it would be like going to a cowboy movie that had no background on the screen that depicted the Old West.

Many of you have memories of Smith's General Store, which was the cultural center of life for those of us who lived in the upper end. But do you remember that Henry had erected a car ramp on the right-hand side of the store that people could drive their car on, then crawl under the ramp and drain the old oil out of their car? This used motor oil was drained into a small barrel and was called by the locals "Burnt oil", and common sense will tell you that sometimes "Burnt oil" is better than no oil at all. Sometimes in summer, it was poured on the gravel road to keep down the dust.

I said all that to tell a very short story I know to be true because I was there when it happened.

Earl Wells owned an old car called a Terraplane, a car built between 1932 and 1938, so it was already an old car at the time of the story. This car had no brakes. So Earl would jamb it into reverse to stop the car. I saw him pull this off on the day of the story. I saw him coming down the hill towards the store. It was a gravel road then and I doubt he could have done what he did had the road been paved, but as he slowed down I saw the car's rear wheels were spinning backwards, throwing up loose gravel.

The only two people who were in the store were one of Henry's sons, Boosie, and me. I remember when two of his sons, William, and Al, came home from WWII, both alive and well. They both soon got new Ford coupe cars, one was yellow, and the other blue. There was another son, Preston, who came home in a casket which they were told not to open. A first cousin of theirs, whom I will not name, once told me he peaked in the casket and only saw an empty uniform, but maybe there was more there you could not see.

Boosie was a good musician and a better one perhaps than he was a storekeeper. He played guitar and sang in a band. Everybody liked him. But just why we called him Boosie I never knew. He always called my mother, Aunt Effie. One of Daddy's sisters was an aunt of his, so he tagged mama as an aunt also.

Anyway, back to Earl and his Terraplane. Earl slid his car to a stop in front the store, got out and came inside, and he asked Boosie. "Boosie, you got any of that burnt oil around?"

Boosie, said, "No Earl, I don't think we do." Earl shrugged his shoulders, turned around, and went back out to his car. As he went around the hood of the car he reached over and patted it, and said, "Sorry honey, guess you'll just have to do without today." And he got in his car and was gone.

Home Is

Home is…
The smell of
Biscuits and gravy,
The warmth of the kitchen,
A table crowded in the corner,
And my mother
Standing at the stove,
Always glad to see me.

Rain Drop Lullaby

A house with an old tin roof
What a blessing when it rained
Especially at night.
No lullaby was ever sung
That sounded half so right.

A metal roof and soft spring rain
Low roll of distant thunder,
Said go to bed you sleepy head,
In a way that worked a wonder.

And while you're snug and dry inside
The cottage roof and walls
Your senses can keep strict account
Of every drop that falls.

You'd snuggle beneath the covers
And just float away to sleep
With peace of mind, I have not found
In a million counted sheep.

Love Can Come in A Box

Shirley and I were married in 1957. We were both still kids. Before a year could pass from our marriage date, we were living in Jacksonville, Florida. We lived there for over 10 years. That proved to be some of the most enjoyable years of our life together. Still, it wasn't perfect because we had moved away from my childhood home and family. We made the trip back home three or four times a year. It was over a 570-mile trip if you came through Atlanta, and took about 14 hours as there were no interstate highways then. It took a long time to cross the state of Georgia, especially after dark, and most of those trips were made after we got off from work. I remember driving at night on the Georgia back roads and seeing humble homes way back off the highway with Christmas trees glowing in the windows, or at times what seemed to be a single lonely blue light.

While living in Florida, one delight we enjoyed was getting a box of Christmas goodies from my Mother every year. Lots of homemade candies, cookies, and my favorite thing, a homemade fruit cake. My wife, when the kids were little, made Christmas goodies too, but she never tried a fruit cake. We are way up in years now and mostly we buy our Christmas goodies, if we have any at all. You can buy a good fruit cake, but not like Mama's. Something is missing from the stuff you buy, and it's love.

But it occurs to me that love can be boxed up and sent in the mail. Also, I know it can because Mama used to box it up and send it to us every Christmas. I know it can because my oldest daughter, Steffany, sent us two boxes this Christmas. We cheated and poked on one until we saw it was jigsaw puzzles, but the other one we saved for Christmas Day. When we opened up that box, love spilled out all over the table. It was filled with homemade Christmas goodies of many different kinds. You would have thought it was gold the way we reacted, but it was better than gold, it was love...that came in a box.

The Rock Hole, A legendary place

It was a hot day in August, temp in the 90s, and stifling! What is a country boy to do? How can you survive this? Boys who lived in Tuckahoe had a ready answer....the Rock Hole! From our house, using shortcuts across the fields, relief was less than a mile away. Gather two or three friends and head out. Get there, strip down to bare naked (nobody owned a bathing suit), jump in the cool water, float around (if you knew how) but no matter, suddenly life was wonderful again.

The Rock Hole is located on the Tuckahoe Creek in the upper end of Tuckahoe. It was, and still is, a great swimming hole. though little used now.

There you will find a large, smooth, limestone rock, projecting out from the south bank, that extends over halfway across the creek. The rock makes a great place to dive or jump from, but it also makes a dam that forces all the stream flow around its north end. The rock dam also causes a small difference between the elevation of the upstream water and the downstream water. All this causes small rocky rapids to flow around the north end of the rock.

That small rapid is why the Rock Hole is a good swimming place. It keeps the sediment and sand swept off the bottom of the creek in this place, which keeps it at a decent depth.

Even so, it was always wise to wade into the swimming hole before you jumped or dove in. Sometimes, after flooding, it would fill up with sand, or you might find a submerged limb or snag.

My dad first took me to the Rock Hole when I was a little kid. There was a tree then on the creek bank just across from "the rock". Some older boys were there climbing up to a low-hanging limb and jumping into the water. I don't know what happened to that tree as it was not there later on.

The rock hole has trees growing around it that provide the privacy needed for bare naked swimming. On the hill above the creek, the house of Bobby Johnson had a view of that whole creek bottom, but not of the Rock Hole. Once when

I and some friends were swimming there, my brother, AB, was fishing nearby. When we were all in the water playing around, he sneaked up and grabbed all our clothes and carried them far out in the field where they could be seen from the house on the hill. If anyone saw us running naked, hunched over, to retrieve our clothes...we never knew.

You don't need to go there to get cool anymore for now we have air conditioning. But sitting in cool conditioned air, though pleasant, does not create a sense of adventure, nor precious memories.

Flooties and Boobies (flu-TIE's & BOO-bee's)

Early spring on our front porch
The sun slips behind the hills,
Supper past, a time for rest, we hear the whippoorwill.
The air was sweet and polished clear, sound traveled on
Such a night
From a distant ridge, a cry resounds!
And breaks the evening quiet.

Was not a wail of grief or pain
But one that touched the heart,
Reminding us that in those days how far folks lived apart.
What message comes from yonder hill?
What means this plaintive cry?
We heard a word, it rose, it fell!
The word
It was—Floo-tie!

L. Clayton Cate

Drifting by on a soft cool breeze
It echoed down the hollows,
And died away in the growing dusk,
We waited for what would follow.
And then from out a red rimmed west,
From the shadows of the trees,
From an unknown voice the answer came,
The answer was—Boo-bie!

And soon with honored quiet between,
From unseen sons and daughters,
Flooties here and Boobies there were
Heard from every quarter.
But as darkness damped the evening light,
Flootie and Boobie ceased.
Silent shined the cold bright stars
Above our hills in peace.

It was an old hill country custom, one that ended long ago.
When folks would holler their lonely out
In the hills of Tuckahoe.
For the Flooties climb no more the hills
Where they once used to call,
And the Boobies are content to stay
Within their roofs and walls.

When the Flooties ceased their calling,
The Boobies voice grew still,
They have returned the clear spring night,
Back to the whippoorwill.
And though I knew every living soul
For miles and miles about
Just who the Flooties and Boobies were,
I never did find out.

The Gardener's Shoes

To what shall I liken life and age?
      Shall I compare it to the day,
Comprised of morning, noon, and night,
      Or seasons marching through the year?
And doubtless each would serve me right,
      Yet both seem tired and overused.
But then I glanced into the mirror,
      And I smiled and thought of shoes.

Shoes, old shoes,
The sort you wear out to the garden
      With all trace of new removed,
With heels run over, soles worn down,
      Laces broken, knotted, frayed,
Which consigned to humble service
      Are like comfortable old friends
You just can't throw away.

For you remember better days.
      Better days when they were new,
When they were strong and sturdy shoes
      Fit for work or walking
With good thick soles for absorbing shock
      For streets both smooth
Or strewn with rock.

And even with too little care
> Proved long and faithful servants.

They do remind me so of life,
> Within conformed to foot and stride,

Without stripped bare of shine or pride.
> But alas, they only reach

That pleasant state…..when the without
> Is pretty much used up.

The War with Sockless

The baseball field behind Ed Jenning's general store was known to every person in Tuckahoe. Most had spent many Saturday afternoons there watching our beloved Pete Dole league baseball team play ball. Tuckahoe always had a good team, plus most of us knew the players by name for most of them were our neighbors.

But sometimes other teams used that field also. Make-up teams from Tuckahoe and other places came to play there. This is a story about one of those games.

Most of our players were teenagers, from both ends of Tuckahoe, upper and lower. I have no memory of the game in question being planned at all. I think the Sockless team just showed up one Saturday wanting to play ball. Most of the players were older than us, and more than that they came with fans to watch, which should have told us this would not be a usual makeup game. It took a while for us to scrounge up enough players to make a team, but eventually, we did.

I was pitching for Tuckahoe, and W.S. was the umpire, and he was standing behind me on the mound as we did not have the protective equipment he needed to stand behind the plate. I remember there was a play on third base where the call did not go our way that upset some of the players on our team, but we let it go. Then after a while, there was an umpire call that upset the Sockless team, and that brought some to the mound to argue with the umpire. It was getting a little heated, so I offered that we had a bad call against us a few minutes earlier and suggested it evened things out. There was a big, and older, Sockless player standing just to my right and when I looked away from him he took a swing at me and hit me with a glancing blow to the jaw. When I looked back he put me in a headlock to prevent me from hitting him. Buddy Brock told me by this time both teams were fighting all over the field. Ed Jennings came down to the field and stopped the fighting. He told the Sockless team to leave the field and to never come back. I found out later that the blow that had glanced off me had hit Monty Elkins right between the eyes and blacked them both.

I had never heard of a place called Sockless, but those players and fans had evidently come from a place up near Dandridge where I found a Sockless Road on a map, But why they came, uninvited, all the way to Tuckahoe to play ball, no one ever explained to me.

Foot Note: I tried to think of the names of the players on our make-up team. There was Delmer Brooks, Clayton Stiles (Nug) Lowell Glen, Don Lane, Buddy Brock, Wayne Russell (Fuzzy), Monty Elkins, Leonard King, and me. It was a long time ago and I may have left some out.

Sadie, A True Dog Story

One sunny day, on a lightly used country lane, a car slows almost to a stop. A door to the car opens and a little dog is thrown out. The car door closes and the car goes on off down the road, picking up speed. The little dog does not run after the car, so perhaps being left beside the road is more to her liking than being in that car. We will never know.

But she trots along in the same direction as the car went and eventually she will come to a house. Perhaps she associates a house with people and food, so she adopts the place. She is a shaggy, scruffy, dirty brown, little female mongrel, and sadly there is nothing attractive about her at all. She is not a dog you would ever pick out to rescue. Still, the man who lives in the house is a kindly soul and when he saw her hanging about, he may have tossed her a scrap of food. She may have been badly treated for she is very shy of him; is not very trusting, or friendly, and would not come near him even when he called to her. If the man gives her food she will not eat it until he leaves. She barks at his neighbors should she see them in the road or in their yards. The man, let's call him Willy, decides to rid himself of the little dog and thinks of calling the dog catcher to take her away. But he has two grandsons who live nearby and they both feel sorry for the little dog and call her Sadie.

Willy does call the dog catcher and they are scheduled to come by the next day to catch her, but that evening Willy has dinner at the home of his grandsons and one of them was asked to say the blessing over the food. The boy, in finishing up his prayer, asks the Lord if he would please remember Sadie and please see that she gets a good home. That was just too much for Willy and he sees he is now stuck with Sadie like it or not.

The next day he somehow caught her, took her to the vet, and had her spayed (Willie may be softhearted, but he is not foolish), then he had her vaccinated and took her home. So, Sadie became the family/neighborhood dog. She doesn't bark at the neighbors anymore, but she will have nothing to do with them. She has become the constant companion of Willy and his extended family, but to nobody else. Wherever Willy goes around his farm, and whether he is mowing the yard or the fields with his tractor, Sadie is always with him. She is still a scruffy little dog, and an outside dog that would not have it any other way. She was an unwanted dog that somehow made a place for herself at a good home, just like in answer to a prayer.

Footnote: Living in the woods as we do it has been our habit to put scraps of food outside in a pan near our back door for whatsoever will to enjoy. Sadie has discovered this and makes a daily trip to our back door to see what fortune will provide. Sadie had a very good Thanksgiving this year.

The Hiding Place

In the short sweet days of summer
Delved deep in the sandridge trace
On a hill both high and lifted up
We made our hiding place.

Was down and down, to the Paw Paw Spring
Then over the Humpback Ridge
Through hollows dark and cross the creek
By way of a deadfall bridge

And it was up we went, and up and up
We forced that laurel hell
Until....until...but, more than that
I swore I'd never tell.

But beneath the dark pines singing
Mid the bush and tangled vine
We tied up sticks, we stacked up stones
And damned the flow of time.

There far removed from parent's eyes
From teachers, books, and school
Was once a kingdom made of three
Where three made all the rules.

The rule we made, there were no rules
To burden hearts and minds
And such a place, a place like that
Proved later hard to find.

We hunt each summer for such a place
By scurrying north and south
But the place we find, while going in
Finds others leaving out.

And my hiding place. I cannot find
One sign of path nor track,
For time has grown, the old ways up
And there is no going back.

And the forest keeps the secret path
That made for the hideout blind
Where a kingdom built of sticks and stones
Was once upon a time.

Attic Bed

Turn my covers down dear mother,
    take me to my attic bed.
Lay me down beneath the rafters
    with the rain soft overhead.
Lay me close beneath the shingles,
    sing me off again to sleep.
Let me feel your hand of caring
    and your kiss upon my cheek.
Bid me dream in sweet reflection,
    sweetly dream of love and home.
Bid me wander wood and meadow
    where a barefoot lad would roam.
O! I'm weary now dear mother
    and I long to see your face.
Long to feel your arms about me
    and the warmth of your embrace.
Come to me now dearest Mother
    fly across the toll of years.
Kneel beside my bed and bless me,
    wipe away the hurt and tears.
I have been so long pretending,
    all the joy is gone from play.
Are there attic beds in heaven
    where an older boy could lay?

River Time

On the grass-lined banks of the river's way
Where the sycamores leaned ore the stream
To catch the light of day,
Or what the shoal upstream might bring,
In youthful bliss, I whiled away the idyllic days of spring.

L. Clayton Cate

It mattered not if day or night
The river bore its broken quiet.
An unseen splash, or the hollow drum
Of an oar on a wooden boat
Would ore the mirrored water float.
The siren laugh of a river daughter
Sound carried well over river water.

On the riverbank in the early morning
Sun jeweled water quietly flowing
Deprived of mankind's useless chatter
I pondered deep and weighty matters
On the origin of things I sometimes mused
Or the better type of bait to use
Though l usually stuck to worms.

But, I did not come to learn
As one might do in church or school
Of algebra, prose, or the golden rule.
Still the river proved a solemn teacher
And more profound than any preacher
On what it had to say,
That my time to fish is very short,
But rivers came to stay.

Snow on the Tuckahoe Hills

We lived on Slemp Road when I was a kid, and when it snowed, I loved to watch cars try to make it up the hill we lived on. It was a nail-biting event. It was a contest between human endeavor and the laws of nature. Who would win out? The outcome was not certain, but the odds were with the hill. It was a long straight road up our hill with no room to get a good run before you hit the grade. It was consistently steep all the way past our house. But, if you made it to the home of Wallace Glenn, there was hope, for by then the hill started to crest and grew less steep the farther you went.

But I had the best seat, all the drama worked out right in front of me. You had better ease off the gas as you went up the hill, for if you ever started spinning the wheels, the game was over, and you were in real trouble. Attempting to back down that hill without sliding out of control was almost impossible.

But that was Tuckahoe in the snow. In an area made up of hills, hollows, and curvy roads, it was trouble no matter which way you went. That didn't seem to bother Smith Store too much. As long as the snow wasn't over the front bumper their old dodge delivery truck would always seem to get through. Pickup trucks are generally not good in the snow, but a little weight in the bed, and with tire chains, they seemed to get where they needed to go   So if you could somehow just make it to Smith Store, Boosie could always get you back home.

It doesn't seem to snow as much here now as it did then, and when six or eight inches of snow was not uncommon. The biggest snow in Tuckahoe I ever saw was over 18 inches. The power was out for about two weeks. But back then, the only thing we really needed power for was lights and the radio, so we got by alright.

If you got out in the fields in that snow, which of course we just had to do, you could get turned around, for the whole world looked different with all the land marks covered up.

Power lines were snapped everywhere by the weight of that snow. And the line from our house to the power pole at Dud King's house was a quarter mile span across cow pastures. When they finally got around to putting that wire back up it was late one evening, the lineman up on the pole by our house was singing "Ghosts Riders In The Sky". He could sing really good, and in the fading light it somehow fit the occasion. I still have that scene, and song, stuck in my mind.

Tuckahoe

Dusty paths were mine to travel,
Wooded hills were there to climb,
Grassy fields I had to ramble,
Hedged with honeysuckle vine.

Now I see the reaching shadows
And the evenings falling fast.
Darkness creeps in all the hollows
And I'm going home at last.

Seems I hear old Noble calling
Far off baying of a hound.
Think he's wanting me to follow
Come and see what he has found.

Somewhere over them high ridges
Must be something really grand.
Fifty years he's had for trailing
Over in the promised land.

Nothing here will I take with me.
I don't need no lantern light.
For the way is straight and narrow,
Ain't no turning left or right.

And a little trail of barefoot tracks
Is all I'll leave to show,
That I wandered for an hour or two
Through a land called Tuckahoe.

Tuckahoe in the Winter
And what was lost

I am now 82 years old, and I feel it, and it occurs to me that I know some things that a lot of you are not old enough to know about. I am not talking about important things but just memories of how it used to be here in Tuckahoe.

Today with all the light from cities, and air pollution, you only see a small fraction in the night winter sky of what we used to see almost every cold winter night; and I remember how very quiet it was. In summer there were the katydids, jar flies, the cicadas, tree frogs, etc., so the nights were full of sounds, but in winter the night was deathly quiet. If a dog was barking on some distant hilltop, miles away, you could clearly hear it. Once in a while, a relative from town would come to visit and spend a winter night. In the morning they would say, "How do you stand it here? It's as quiet as death!"

But there were some sounds to be heard if you had ears to hear, and happened to be outside. At Strawberry Plains, about 10 miles from Tuckahoe, there is a railroad, and there has been since the days before the Civil War. At night a freight train would pass through Strawberry Plains and you could hear, almost feel, the sound of the wheels on the rails, and far off in the dark would come the long low moan of the train's steam whistle. And I wish I could somehow write the sound of it, but that is beyond the power of the written word. Also, at times, if the wind was right, you could hear trucks traveling on Asheville Highway, a good six miles away.

And although it made no sound, there was the house mountain beacon light. Every few seconds or so it would sweep around clockwise through the night sky. Though I never knew its purpose I supposed it was for guidance of airplanes.

And, Lordy, the stars, the number of stars you could see on a clear winter night was breathtaking. The Milky Way, our home galaxy, composed of billions of stars, appeared as a cloud-like band stretching across the night sky and could be easily seen; today you would have to travel to a desolate place, far from city lights and air pollution, to see what we saw every night. We saw "the heavens really do declare the glory of God and show His handiwork".

All this comes to mind because A few years back we made a trip to Death Valley with some friends. It was late fall and cool, so we made a long day of it, and by the time we left the park, it was pretty dark. We had just gotten back on the highway toward Las Vegas when I suddenly remembered something that I had read, and called out, "Stop the car!" We pulled off to the side of the highway and we all got out of the car and looked up...and we just stood there with our mouths open. The night sky was blazing with stars beyond belief. We were far removed from any city lights and air pollution, and I had the thought, the night sky once looked much like this in Tuckahoe.

L. Clayton Cate

The Country Church

Mary's Door

A mystery borne on ethereal wings,
Was mercy carried to extremes?
Was it an Angel or a dream
That came to Mary's door?

A star that guides the wise by night
Who brought both gold and good advice
That Joseph flee with son and wife.
Death hunts for Mary's door.

A voice that cries from the wilderness
The powers of darkness come to test.
Is this one different from the rest,
Of all who came before?

The people cry, a sign! a sign!
They eat His bread, they drink His wine,
They say we see, but they are blind
To the light from Mary's Door.

Who breaks the seal, who now unfolds
What prophets from the past foretold?
That God intends to cleanse the soul
By way of Mary's door.

Her son is raised above the earth.
He pays much more than we are worth
His blood is mingled with the earth
In front of Mary's door.

A body lies in a borrowed tomb
That she once carried in her womb.
And grief has come and all too soon
To live at Mary's door.

The golden dawn of a glorious day,
The tomb is empty now they say.
And hope has come where no hope lay
Last night at Mary's door.

A love so great it has reversed
The scarlet of an age-old curse.
The one who brought grace down to earth
Came out from Mary's door.

A virgin blessed with favor from
The great I AM who sent His son.
The Son of God indeed has come
Come out of Mary's door.

This Christmas message now resounds
Through every hamlet, every town,
Has spread the entire world around,
Away from Mary's door.

Humble Pie

Peter denied the Lord three times
        before the cock could crow;
        he cursed and swore that Jesus was
        a man he did not know.

Before that in the garden
        this man had shown no fear,
        where defending Jesus with his sword,
        he cut off a fellow's ear.

I think he would have stood up there
        at least he would have tried
        for there is a glory for the hero
        even if the hero dies.

But there is no glory in the cross
        by the multitude reviled,
        and to die with murders and thieves
        was just not Peter's style.

Do you love me, Simon Peter?
        was three times for Jesus, too,
        and three times Peter answered him
        oh Lord, you know I do.

It must be hard to face a friend
        a friend you have betrayed
        when he stood in peril of his life
        and you just walked away.

But pride must go before a fall
        and I think Peter fell;
        but how sweet to fall at Jesus' feet
        instead of into hell.

My friends, there is a lesson here,
        for Adam's sons and daughters,
        who never faced death on a cross
        and never walked on water.

A Poor Man's House

Have you ever dropped into a poor man's house
    when the wind blew hard and chill?
Have you ever dropped into a poor man's house
    when the day was warm and still?

Have you held the hand of a poor man's child
    while the poor man spoke his grace?
Have you ever seen tears, while he thanked the Lord,
    roll down on a poor man's face?

Have you ever seen care on a poor man's face
    while you sat in the poor man's seat?
Have you ever sat down at a poor man's plate
    and took of the poor man's meat?

Have you ever seen Christ on a poor man's wall
        smile down on the poor man's lot?
Have you ever went home and down on your knees
        gave thanks for the life you've got?

Have you wondered why, when the Lord came down,
        why he walked in the poor man's shoes?
Have you ever had the thought, that the more you get,
        it's more that you've got to lose?

Have you ever cried out, Lord, let me see,
        see the tears that the poor man cries?
Such as you did when you chose to look
        at the world through a poor man's eyes.

Adam's Hand

Mother was sitting in her rocker
And as she sang a little tune,
Her small weak voice, unknowing, cast
Long shadows cross the room.

"My buddy, oh my buddy,
No buddy.... quite so true."
And so it went, and ended with
"Your buddy... misses you."

That her thoughts were of my father
It was not hard to guess,
Though fifteen years at least had passed
Since he was laid to rest.

Those years had not been kind to her
With her body bowed and bent.
Now those that kept the house and farm,
To rock, must be content.

It was hard to see resemblance
To the person in the chair,
In the picture on the mantle,
Of a girl so young and fair.

Those days of gold had passed away
They would not come again.
How tragic is our lot in life,
To lead to such an end.

I do not doubt thy wisdom, Lord.
You prophesied such sorrow,
And warned us that we should not count
On riches or tomorrow.

For such an end must come to all
Who toil beneath the sun.
As from this gift, from Adam's hand,
There is no place to run.

L. Clayton Cate

Fires in the Wildwood

"It was a tiny congregation - seldom more than thirty souls,
You could count 'em every Sunday,
As they come walk'n down the roads.
To a humble little building
They had made with their own hands,
A sort of sacrifice to Jesus - from His small devoted band.
It had a tin roof with a belfry,
And wood side'n painted white
And was turned to greet the sunrise -
Which they all agreed was right.
It had an alter for repent'n - and a pulpit for the bold,
With a kneeling place for sinners
For convert'n of the soul.

Someone would come in early, build a fire
And ring the bell,
A sound that sweetened up the valley,
Ever' holler, hill and dale
For it proclaimed that it was Sunday
And it was time for gett'n fed
For the note that rang - was calling out
The liv'n from the dead.
Old brother King would start the service
With a rouse'n joyous song
And from grandpas down to babies
All the rest would sing along.

You could hear them folks rejoicing
From a mile or so away,
With no apologizing for the things that they might say.

And that preacher he was going
Where the spirit must have led
For he wasn't one for preach'n
What he'd thought up in his head.
Soon he'd get all hot and sweaty
Then he'd shuck his coat and tie
And he'd aim the word right at you
While he looked you in the eye.
And you'd be sorry you was sinful
So you'd go up to make it right,
Which might cause a celebration
Last'n deep into the night.
Then they'd ask for testimonies
That the faithful there could use

And the flock was all so grateful
Hardly one of them refused.
And some sister might start shouting
Which would usual start a fire,
Leaping pews was kinda common
Wouldn't hardly rate a stare.

No, it wasn't they was better
Why they had a cause to shout,
It was joy, so welled inside'em they just had to let it out.

Course them days are all behind us
And might never come again.
Now the buildings are real splendid
That the faithful gather in.
And the bell? it's sitt'n silent
Been retired into the grass
And the service ain't offending
If a soul should wander past.
Now we're refined and educated with a full-up parking lot,
And we were all infatuated with the finery that we got.
We got a preacher down from Boston
With a string of them degrees,
And that carpet made the alter
Mighty pleasant on the knees.
And we got the service scheduled,
With a scheduled time to end,
With ever-thing in perfect order,
And we're sticking to the plan.

You'd think that we'd be happy
That the Lord has blessed us so,
But we keep so quiet about it
How's a body s'posed to know?"
Here the elder brother paused - took a breath
And heaved a sigh,
And with a kerchief from his pocket,
Wiped the memories from his eyes.

For the church was deadly quiet
From the front row to the rear,
And the feelings ran the gamut from astonishment to tears.
And the brothers hair was raise'n
On the neck behind his head,
So he was quick to guess correctly
It was something that he said.
And in trying hard to fix it, ere returning to his seat,
He stuck in this addendum which is worthy to repeat.

"I hope - I ain't accused of judg'n,
And I hope that I ain't right,
For I hope that we are pleasing in the Holy Father's sight,
And if organized and quiet is the way we ought to be,
Then he ought to be some happy for we got it to a tee.

But…I'm just fondly recollect'n,
I don't mean to cause no stir,
I'm just thinking on…. the way things are…
And remembering…how they were."

God's Gift

My ship a sturdy craft she is,
    and flying every sail.
She has the bit between her teeth
    and leans into the gale.

And I upon the rolling deck
    am up to greet the sun,
And every wave beneath the bow
    I've relished, every one.

Til sailing eastward all the day,
    we leave the sun behind,
And on the wake our good ship makes,
    it lays a fiery shine.

Still, strike we not a single sail.
    And dark becomes a boon.
The stars wink on and by their light
    we rush to meet the moon.

The Captain, steadfast by the helm,
    his faithful vigil keeps.
He is a bold and fearsome soul
    who has no need of sleep.

And loath I am to quit the deck
    I've grown to love it so.
Too soon the bell will sound the hour
    that sends my watch below.

But now I see, I feel, I hear,
    it is a gift sublime.
For all that is cries, No! Not now,
    and nowhere down the line.

Such Is

If paradise be found a place
Of flowering tree and golden field,
Of rivers running clear and free,
Of fruit and berry laden vine,
Of constant spring and summer time,
Of blue-sky days and starry nights,
And free of things that sting and bite.
Then wouldn't it be nice to be
A child again in heaven.
For I grow tired of these old bones
And this old house of mine.
And I would be a child and live
With Jesus all the time.

Looking for You

In the dark of the night, down in old Carolina,
I was searching the stations, you know how you do,
And I happened to hit on this old country preacher
And I heard him cry "Jesus is looking for you."

He said, I'm not sent to judge you, my brother,
And I'll not keep you long, I'm just passing through.
But he told me search, the highways and hedges.
Yes, "Jesus has sent me out looking for you."

He's looking for you, yes, looking for you.
I've no fancy words, and no begging I do.
My orders are short, He sent me out searching.
Yes, "Jesus has sent me out looking for you."

He said the sheep and the goats are all mingled together.
And not mine to divide or tell who is who.
But His sheep know his voice and He said they would answer,
If I'd call out that "Jesus is looking for you."

Do you hear a sweet voice, do you hear Jesus calling,
calling you home? Here's what you must do.
Just call on His name, He promised He'd answer.
Since you wandered away, "He's been looking for you."

Then he said a short prayer and his sermon was over
and he told me good night, as no more could he do.
But I'm thankful today that he dared the dark valley
To tell me that "Jesus is looking for you."

If'n Jesus Wuz

If'n Jesus had just a-wanted to,
he'd a-give it up on me and you,
And they'd not been no crown o' thorns
or spear to pierce his side.

Had'nt he not been so full of love
he'd a-give this world a great big shove,
Sent ever-thing that ever was
out on a roar'n tide.

Or if'n Jesus, he'd a-been like me
They'd a-shore not hung him on no tree.
He'd a-called right down from heaven's shore
them fiercest angel bands.

They'd a-cleaned up this old earth-ez floor
they'd a-swept thuh trash right out thuh door.
Then fetched him back to glory land
where he wuz appreciated.

Course - that ain't the way - that Jesus wuz
'Cause Jesus, He wuz full o' love
And thuh job that God had sent him fer,
At's thuh job he would abide.

So he spilled it out, his precious blood,
Run down that cross, right in the mud,
Might uh got some on that soldier's toe,
Might uh saved his onery hide.

Fer he was'nt like us, and that's a-fact,
He had the stuff we humans lack.
Goodly stuff, like self control,
Fer times when it would matter.

Fer if'n Jesus, He'd a-been like us,
Why, He'd a-bought his-self a great big bus
Painted Jesus and thuh twelve apostles
In big letters on thuh sides.

Or he might uh had a TV show
Fer rak'n in big piles o' dough.
Maybe built his-self a mansion house
and filled it up with pride.

Yeah, if"n Jesus had-a-been like me and you
That's the kinda things he'd likely do,
Fer that's thuh stuff folks care about
Who walk thuh worldly way.

A Little Short

I rode upon a great white horse,
A knight who fought for good.
In every act I thought was right
I did the best I could.

Oh God, of all the earth and sea,
And all the heavens high,
Have mercy on those precious souls
Whose hope was such as I.

Cause for Celebrat'ng?

Centennial year, the pastor said,
        a cause for celebration!
He informed us here last Sunday morn,
        the entire congregation.

He told us of the planned events.
        He thought we ought to know.
How the old folks used to worship here
        a hundred years ago.

Our choir sang a rousing special
        in their tailored robes of blue.
They sang a song I had not heard
        that had a catchy tune.

They sing so good it made me wish
        they'd sing a song I know,
The kind of song they might have sung
        a hundred years ago.

Then the church got awful quiet
        when the preacher took the stand
And it made a feller wonder
        if he ought to say "amen."

And the Bible he was reading,
        it ain't like the one I know.
I doubt that they'd a took to that
        a hundred years ago.

I don't question we've made progress
        but I think we've lost some too,
And if the trade was good or bad
        I'll leave that up to you.

But I kinda miss the shout'n
        and the tears of joy that flowed
When the folks got in the spirit here
        a hundred years ago.

It's not that they were better
        and did everything they ought,
They were just happy Jesus saved 'em
        and forgave them of their faults.

And so much joy welled up inside 'em
        it just had to overflow,
I'll bet they scared some sinners here
        a hundred years ago.

Lazarus at the Gate

Or my experience as a bell ringer

"There was a certain rich man"...that's the way the parable starts, and it goes on to tell of a poor man outside the rich man's gate. The beggar's existence was dependent on the crumbs that fell from his table. I have volunteered to take the place of the beggar for a few hours today. I will "ring the bell" for the Salvation Army.

I have been assigned to man the 2 to 4 P.M. shift in front of Dillard's at the Knoxville Center Mall. I arrive fifteen minutes early and find a lady bell ringer there with her two small children. I am her replacement. Her little daughter is tired and cranky, and I offer to start early so she can take her home. She accepts and seems grateful. I take over ten minutes early.

My instructions are simple: stand beside the alms bucket, be courteous, be cheerful, dress neatly and warmly, and ask for nothing. Just smile and "ring the little bell." So, I ring it, I smile, and I greet, express thanks, bless people, open doors, and the minutes tick away.

After a short while, the thought occurs to me that this is a little like being God. You see this one gives a tad, that one a tad more, and that one passes by on the other side of the road (the door down on the end). It's not that you are making an effort to watch behavior; you just can't help but notice. I find that I can almost tell when people exit their cars if they will give something. You realize you are in danger of being judgmental. So, you tell yourself that you don't know these people; you can't see into their hearts or know what they have or have not done.

OK, but then you wonder what do you do with your eyes? Do you look at people as they approach? Will that be interpreted as expecting them to donate? Maybe I should just stare at the distant ridge? No, that won't work. I don't want to stand here like a statue. And what about the bell? Should I ring it fast or slow? Should I wait until someone approaches and then start ringing? No, I can't do that as that would be like saying, "Here comes one, better get a ring on just for them." No, I decide it must ring at all times, even when I can't see a soul. That way when someone drives up and opens their car door they will hear the bell and know it is not ringing just for them even though it is. *"Ask not for whom the bell tolls, it tolls for thee"*. Why did I think of that? I decide to ring the bell in time with Jingle Bells.

"It rains on the just and unjust alike," that is how God is, and in a small way I am His emissary, so I decide I will speak kindly and open doors for those who donate as well as for those who don't. If people pass by close to me, I will

open the door for them and greet them. If they give something I will also say, "God bless you," and otherwise, just say "Good afternoon.". If they choose the far door I will not bother them.

A nicely dressed lady, walking quickly, exits the store; she is tall, thin, and wearing slacks. She has on mid-height shoes, the kind with thick heels. The heels make a, pop, pop, pop, noise as she walks. Why do I find that sound pleasant?

I wonder what the money I am collecting will be used for? How would I answer if someone asks me? I trust that it will be used to help the poor at Christmas. To some, it will be a blessing. Will they all deserve it? No, probably not, but then what has deserving got to do with the spirit of giving? It's not about getting what we deserve; it's about compassion and mercy. None of us want to get what we deserve, at least not from God. I do know some people will need help, I am certain of it! Besides that, it is a useless thing for me to worry about. I trust the Salvation Army, or I wouldn't be here.

I decide that the real blessing is in the giving and I am offering people an opportunity to share in that blessing. Some people seem to get it as they walk up smiling, and they leave smiling. Some just drop in money with a grunt. I "God bless" them anyway. An elderly black lady, who looks as though she could use some financial help herself, drops in two dollars. I think of the widow's mite. I think God smiled at that, I know I did.

A mother and little boy come by. How cute! She is going to let him put in the coins. He drops in one, and then another, and then puts his hand under the bucket and peers underneath. His mother supposes he is looking for a gumball to drop out.

I think what a clever idea this bell ringing is: this just standing here, being pleasant, and ringing a little bell. You don't have to look at me, but you can't ignore the ringing bell. Your ears won't let you get away with it.

There are six doors at this entrance to Dillard's. I am stationed near the eastern most. You can pass me by and enter by the western most (and some people do), but my bell will greet you when you get out of your car, come with you to the door, and follow you through into the vestibule. It will stay in the back of your mind while you are shopping. You ask yourself, "Do I want to go back out that way and pass that bell ringer again?" You perhaps think I am judging you, but I am not. You are judging yourself. A good idea, this little bell.

I find some people do think you are judging them. Some quickly say, "I already gave", or "Catch you on the way out", or "I sent a check." I thank them. I told one lady who seemed especially flustered, "I don't pass judgment. I just ring the bell".

I am the only bell ringer in all of Knoxville Center Mall and the other nearby stores. That's a little scary. A Salvation Army van stopped, and the driver told me I was the only one. I only stand a two-hour shift and I wonder if I will have a replacement. I find I am hoping I will. I find I don't like the idea that nobody will be here. It is a beautiful, if cool day, but luckily I am facing south. The sun is playing hide and seek in a blue sky full of lacy white clouds, so I am warm one minute and cool the next. Bordering the parking lot are rows of bushes with blood red foliage. Across the access road are several Bradford pears in full multi-color splendor. The air is fresh and delightful to breathe. What a fine day the Lord has made!

It's strange but I am beginning to care more about the people I see. A lady smoking a cigarette approaches. I have a sudden desire to advise her to quit: to tell her about my brother who died of lung cancer; about a fellow Sunday school member who is now being treated for the same af fliction, and of a sister-in-law who must use oxygen all the time. I decide against doing that. I am not here to change society, just to ring a bell.

I find I admire the young mothers who come shopping with small kids in tow. I know it took some doing to make that happen. Wow! That lady that just passed sure smelled good!

An elderly fellow stops to chat. He would never give to the Red Cross, he opines, but he will give to the Salvation Army. He tells of his experience when debarking a troopship in England in '42 or '43, he is not sure which. "I was sick all the way over," he says. "Never ate a bite, couldn't!" He went on, "When we arrived, there was a Salvation Army booth on the dock. They were serving tea, coffee, sausage, and biscuits, and it sure was good. We were there to get ready for D-Day," he continued. I looked at him, "You were in the D-Day invasion!" I asked. "Yes I was," he said. "Been back twice since then." I shook his hand.

Cars, trucks, vans, and SUV's, of all makes, models, ages, and condition, come and go in the parking lot. Some, as Dillard's is an upscale store, are very expensive models. I find I am not envious of any of them. But then I am tested. Into the lot zips a little black Porsche roadster. It has a lady driver. No! No!!! I think. Don't squeeze in that little space between those two cars! But she does anyway (were it mine I would shoot my wife for doing that). I realize I have broken the law. I am COVETING. I ring the bell slow and solemnly. I think the rich man must have had to pass by Lazarus every day. He couldn't avoid seeing him. I wonder if Jesus was really talking about literal crumbs?

Earlier I noticed that someone had left their lights on, and it bothers me. Dimmer and dimmer they get as time passes by.

I have hummed a lot of carols today. "And on every street corner you hear." Hmmm...I wonder if the song "Silver Bells" is about Salvation Army bell ringers? But my bells not silver, it's red. Oh well. My two hours are almost up, and I don't see anyone who looks the part of a volunteer. My shift is up and still no replacement. I stay an extra fifteen minutes and then I know I must go. It is the Tuesday before Thanksgiving and I have several stops to make before I can go home. With a little sadness I take down the bucket, fold up the stand, and place it inside the vestibule. I take the bucket and leave it at the customer service desk. I leave the store by way of the door where I stood my shift. I feel a little like a deserter. I decide I will come back.

I realize I did not do a perfect job. I did not open the door for every soul. I doubt if I properly thanked every person who gave. I probably did do some judging even though I tried not to. I will try to do better when I return. And then I have a thought, "I can practice doing that without having to ring a bell." Maybe I am beginning to get it, too.

I have done two more shifts since then, have two more on schedule, and I may do more. There are several other duties I could volunteer for, but bell ringers are needed the most right now. It is front line duty, the foot soldiers, and I find I enjoy doing it. Go figure.

"Merry Christmas and God Bless You." I just couldn't help doing that.

A Simple Man

God made me a simple man.
I've not much wealth to show,
But flowers smell as sweet for me
As anyone I know.

The stars shine just as bright on me
As the king of any land.
And I feel cheated not a whit
To be a simple man.

Of knowledge I have little store
And fame has passed me by.
If I were not so simple, I
Suppose that I'd know why.

But God He gives me bread enough
To keep my family fed.
And blesses us with roof and cots
On which to lay our heads.

And in the morning garden,
I hear buzzing of the bees,
And I hear the song birds singing
From their nests among the trees.

And my heart gets near to bust'n
From the glory of the land.
It's apt to make a soul forget
He's just a simple man.

And I'm think'n 'bout, when God came down
To show himself our friend,
From manger to the rugged cross,
I see a simple man.

I ain't saying that I measure
To that Man from Galilee,
But maybe He was showing us
The way we ought to be.

Fer like as not that you'd forget,
If wealth was in your hands,
Your heart its beat'n in your breast
Just like the simple man's.

Power in the Book

As the preacher paced behind the old pulpit
His steps made the wood floor creak
While on the fifth bench back
On the window side, old Lige
Was fast asleep.

The preacher, he spoke on the fire of hell
And his up raised fist he shook
His sweat ran down,
He was all worked up
And he pounded on the book.

And I guess it wouldn't stretch the truth
To 'low he was upset
That old Lige could stay
Through the threat of hell
So peacefully at rest.

But he might have come to the usual end
though he was stirred - down to his core,
But it was just too much
At the alter call
When Lige began to snore

Well, the preacher grabbed up that Holy Book
And he hurled it out in space
Aimed true and hard
At the fifth bench back
At Lige's blissful face.

But fate stepped in and Lige slumped down
And the good book sailed on by
And made a di'rect hit
On sister Sarah Kitts
Right square between her eyes.

Though her scream might not have woke the dead
It was enough to wake up Lige
But he plumb mistook
Her screams of pain
For a shout'n joyous cry.

For the Preacher was up there running 'round
And 'a crying, "Lord I'm sorry!"
And the jumping people
All seemed spirit filled
In their zeal to help poor Sarah.

Well, that was just too much for old Lige to bear
and conviction wrenched his soul
and he leaped from the bench
crying, I repent!
And he lost all self-control.

And all the people wept at the Joy they felt
That his soul was saved from sin
And Sara's two black eyes?
Seemed a small sacrifice
To give for a soul to win

Well, that meeting is one that's still talked about
For they all moved up that night
When the power in the book
Got a whole church shook
When the preacher aimed it right.

Farther Out

Wet Wood

One tiny, frail, and glowing spark,
Can start a great devouring fire
That can eat away a forest
In a race of wild desire.

And go leaping over mountains
Consuming all that's in its path
With the wind a boon companion
Doing all the fire asks.

But no fire however raging
Concerns the mighty thunder storm.
Its flame is tied and bound to earth
And poses it no harm.

And the fire is not so hungry
When the wood is soaking wet!
And though this poem should have a moral
The poet hasn't found it yet.

So, I'll conclude it here by saying,
Though it's not without a doubt,
May the storm that you are dreading
Put your present troubles out.

I Am

If time is stretching as a line
Extending ever on
Through a vast and eternal spreading sky,
Never ending or beginning,
Where am I?

If ages numberless have passed
Long ere I was conceived,
And numberless are waiting
Still to be,
Why now me?

If on this tiny sphere of earth
Men have so long been dwelling,
Princes reigned in pomp and splendor
And then died,
Where was I?

If in this starry field
Which reaches out forever
I am existing in some corner as a spot,
My knowing makes me different,
Does it not?

Then the greatest of all things
In this universe I see,
Though works of many wonders do abound,
The greatest thing is knowing
That I am.

Needful Things

The last words
I heard my Father say
As I stood beside his bed
In that antiseptic world called ICU…
And of all the things
I would rather do than remember…
But, sadly, neither had prescience
Enough to say…
The needful things.

Twilight World

In a twilight world, in static air,
A doll sits still as stone.
The days sweep by, the seasons pass
Outside her attic home.

Her dress is laced by spider's web, her shoes
Are gone from style.
Yet she retains a grace, and still a trace,
Of rosy painted smile.

She abides in somber stillness as
A ray of sunbeam fair,
Strikes through motes of floating dust
And lights her golden hair.

She is a beauty far past her prime
But she harbors no regret.
Her arms untiringly have reached
To emptiness and yet,

No heart has broke inside her breast, no tears
Have dimmed her eyes.
She bore no sad and parting words
Nor burden of good-bye.

So love and pity are wasted here,
And are useless to bestow.
No....those in need of things like that
Dwell in the rooms below.

Nature's brew

Down to the stream
The robin came
To partake of the brew
That nature wrings
From clouds in spring
To compliment the dew.

Wished Away

When one is very, very young
The hours seem to pass as slow
As water wears a rock, and
A clock is just a curious thing
That only says, "Tick Tock."

It's only when you enter school
That time begins to gain control
And start its long domain.
For knowing when to wake or sleep
Becomes a needful thing.

Then come the years you bend to work
To every task an hour assigned,
And time becomes your master.
A love and hate relationship,
And the ticks are getting faster.

This morning at an early hour,
I rubbed the sleep out of my eyes
And got a gentle shock.
I looked to see what my clock said
But, it only said "Tick Tock."

"Tick Tock, Tick Tock, Tick Tock, Tick Tock,"
I scratched my head and listened hard.
But, "Tick Tock" was all it said.
It offered no advice at all,
So I returned to bed.

How many hours I've wished away
From my allotted time.
An old habit I have stopped.
I'd like to wish them back again,
"Tick Tock, Tick Tock, Tick Tock."

Bone of My Bone

Look back, look back,
See yet the brook, the fruitful vine,
The garden.
See here the blood red rose that blows
The promise of the pardon.

Bone of my bone,
Flesh of my flesh, l took thee there
My helper
And pledged my troth with thee to walk
Forever and forever.

Til the rising sun
Shall fail at last, and rivers
Cease from flowing,
My heart and thine shall be entwined
As long as grass is growing.

Til we shall stand
Before that bar, but standing still
Together
Before the One who made the bond
That only He can sever.

What Love Is

Once I met the most fetching woman I thought I had ever seen. Her face, her form, her eyes, I couldn't help thinking about. I was sure it was love. Later, we met again, we talked, later still, we kissed. Even later, we held each other tight all through one sultry summer night. I thought for certain that was love.

Then came the day we parted, when she just walked away and left me holding on to air. My heart ached so. I thought I'd surely die of love. But I didn't, so maybe it wasn't love. And to all you lovers out there who are pining for someone you never really knew, or who have lost someone you never really had, and who tried to care for one, who didn't care for you, I know how you feel, it's bad, I've felt that, too. But is that love?

But I once knew an old man of a gentle, tender mind, who, while walking through his life chanced upon a small and beautiful baby bird which somehow had lost its mother. It needed someone to care for it, so he picked it up and took it home. The little bird thought he was its mother and it snuggled up close to his heart.

He fed the little bird by hand, and later on, even taught it how to fly. But only around inside his house, for he knew the world outside his house was a dangerous place for a little bird to be. And the little bird was happy and it sang to him, It brightened up his life. And an old man can use a little brightness in his life. It made him happy, too.

But still he knew that little birds don't belong inside of houses. And he tried hard not to think about that but he did anyway for he knew that little birds should not live inside of places with walls and roofs and windows. And shouldn't be living with old men, who couldn't give them what they really needed to have. So, one fine spring morning he walked to his window with the little bird in his hand and even as his heart cried out "Oh No!" he opened the window, and he opened his hand.

And the little bird flew out and up into the wide blue sky. He watched as it tried its wings. It soared and dived and then he watched as it flew away. He stood there at the window, smiling and crying, for a very long while and he wondered how it was possible that one could feel sad and happy at the same time. And he thought, "This must be what love is like." Finally, he closed the window, turned back into the room, walked out into his kitchen and made some toast. But his heart stayed outside, soaring and dipping in the bright spring air.

A Lover's Touch

Just two feet over
In a king size bed
On a snow soft pillow
Lies my lover's head.
In the dark I reach
And I touch her hair
I can't feel red
Still, I know it's there.
But I do feel love
Love sure and deep.
My foot finds hers
And I fall asleep.

Of Interpretation

As a flood, his feelings
Struggled within his breast
Trying to burst forth
To sweep over her
To drown her in
His love.

He longed
To tell her of the fire
The wondrous bliss
She stirred within him
For he was drunk
From the new wine
Of passions heady brew
And ardor's vintage kiss.

But, alas! he was such
A simple lad
Not learned in word or way
He formed the unsayable
Inside his mouth
But "I love you" ...trembling out
Was all that he could say.

Which seemed to him not
Nearly good enough that night
But she...she thought it was,
Answered back again,
And held on tight.

Near to Home

In the forest deep, an old fire ring
I came upon, of blacked stone,
Where once had been a rendezvous,
Where warmth once was that now is gone.

And I suppose I could have stopped
Had I been blessed with time to spare,
And gathered up old coals enough
To see how a new flame might fare.

But time no longer was my friend
And starting fires to no avail
For I am now too near my home
For spending nights out on the trail.

If You Think of Me

Should some evening find you strolling
By an ivied garden wall,
Should you chance to catch the sunrise
At some lovely water fall.
Should the birds be serenading
So the woods are filled with song
In a world so full of wonder,
Will you miss me when I'm gone?

Let not the beauty of the garden
Be concealed by sad repose,
Nor the promise in the sunrise
Be as faded as the rose
That has met the frost of winter
That has chilled it to the bone.
Will my thought become a burden?
Will you miss me when I'm gone?

Let me not become a shadow
Casting darkness o'er the light,
Stealing as a ghostly presence
Haunting all your days and nights.
I would be a breeze refreshing,
Cool and gentle off the sea,
That can wrap a smile around you,
If you chance to think of me.

Sweet on Me

Sarah Jo was sweet on me,
But I was sweet on Sally,
But she was sweet on Billy Bob,
Who lived some down the alley.

And he was sweet on Wilma Jean,
And she was sweet on him,
So love and luck filled Billy's cup
A little past the brim.

Well, Sarah married later on,
I never found to who,
And Sally married Jimmy Smith,
A thing she had to do.

Just two of us were all that got
The one they hoped to get,
And I'm still looking for Sally's twin,
But I haven't found her yet.

And life's not been the fairy tale
It's painted up to be,
For the one that I was sweetest on,
She wasn't sweet on me.

Mmmmm!

I once knew a darling little girl,
Not yet able to articulate her thoughts
Because of her tender years.
But old enough to say simple words,
Old enough to call me "Papaw."

I remember driving in our car
With her in the back seat.
I remember her calling "Papaw!"
And I would answer "What?"
And she would say, "Mmmmm!"

And smile the sweetest smile,
And her, "Mmmmm!"
Made me smile, too.
She is a little older now
And talks much better.

She still sits in the back seat
When we drive in our car.
And she still calls out "Papaw!"
And I still answer, "What?"
But now she says, "I love you!"
And I say, "Mmmmm!"

Papaw Blues

The task I am assigned today is sitt'n my granddaughter,
To not get wood, to not tend fire, and not to carry water.

But, I've advice from stem to stern
For all the stuff I ought'er,
Had better not, and better had, to care
For my granddaughter.

With lots of this and tons of that, of every sort and kind,
And almost every bit is used to care for her behind.

With cockle shells and awful smells from little bits of poop,
And sippy-cups and spittin-up and sorry at-tee-tudes.

And Lordy, all that tiny stuff she's find'n on the floor.
I pulled some stuff, from that kid's mouth,
I've never seen before.

Then finally, worn down to a nub, she drifted off to sleep.
For almost fifteen minutes there, she never made a peep.

And I had sit me down a spell, to take a needed rest,
Then she woke up with such a yell,

L. Clayton Cate

It scared me half to death.
I got her safe and buckled in and eat'n in her chair,
And half of what she had was eat, and half was in her hair.

Then all washed down and slickered up,
And with a change O' clothes,
I spent the afternoon with her, uh play'n piggy toes.

And she was just as full o' life and gave me such a smile,
She paid her old granpappy back,
And made it worth the while.

When they got back at even'n from their
Shoppin' at the mall,
Her stuff had overflowed the room and skittled up the hall.

An some of granny's stuff was broke,
But most was only cracked,
And I was bent and ach'n from a play'n piggyback.

And then they had the nerve to ask,
While plow'n thru' the rubble,
Did you and little bit have fun and was she any trouble?

Ah, but I've learned a lesson here of legendary order
To never volunteer alone to care for my granddaughter.

Disposable Love

I just came in from the country.
        I was young and I was green.
Just an empty-headed dreamer
        who was searching for his dream.
Who found love on every corner
        on the shady sides of town,
For no deposit, no return—and nothing down.

Ain't it strange how in the city
        you won't know a soul you meet.
But there's love there for the asking
        on the dark side of the street.
It don't ask you 'bout tomorrow.
        it don't need no wedding gown.
It's no deposit, no return—and nothing down.

When I went back to the country
        it was with a heavy load,
And I couldn't help but notice
        all the trash along the road.
All them colored plastic bottles
        just old empties turning brown,
From no deposit, no return—and nothing down.

L. Clayton Cate

I don't tell this story often
    of the time I was a fool,
And the lessons learned by living
    that they never taught in school.
If you want a love that's lasting,
    well, it ain't the kind that's found,
For no deposit, no return—and nothing down.

Two Travelers

These last eighteen months, I have watched my granddaughter grow, advancing from sitting, to crawling, to walking and only lately with much determined coaching, learning how to talk, and I am reminded of a time when I was once creeping forward myself restrained by the densest type of fog, feeling my way across central Florida in the early morning dark.

Helplessly, I had watched as the world I knew slowly contracted to the dimly lit interior space of my car, beyond whose windows nothing existed, except gray, damp oblivion, laced with the bitter odor of burning peat from some distant bog fire. The light from the headlamps, rendered useless by the thick soup, I opened the car door and looked down at the pavement. It was still there. There was comfort in that.

Following the painted center line, visible below the open door, I crept forward into the unknown in the hope that somewhere ahead would be the larger world I knew, and so it was about ten minutes later. But not all at once, for it is the way of fog to capture and let go slowly as it also was once.

I watched others, returning, day by day, into that darker fog from which we all escaped, dropping the hard-won tools of life, one by one along the way. So do travelers pass in the misty part of life, one emerging, one dissolving, and are unaware, as my granddaughter is unaware. She is at that solitary time, when one proceeds forward to all ahead, and nothing leaves behind.

Usetabees

The outlaws were all shown their place
The wrong was set to right
And a red sunset was waning fast
When he turned in for the night.

And as heroes do, both small and great,
He bids his friends good-bye,
And homeward comes a silhouette
Hard-edged against the sky.

My trail-wise little cowboy bold,
Whose aim is true and sure,
With his broom tailed steed, a winning smile,
And motives good and pure.

God bless thee my little buck-a-roo.
May your heart be always so.
But the time is come to lay down your gun
To bath and bed you go.

But should you cross trails, in slumber land,
with those outlaw Usetabees
And a jug-jawed man with a bad gun hand,
They might remember me.

For I knew those boys some years ago
In a day that's long since gone.
You might tell them for me, should they ask,
Why I've stayed away so long.

The News

The news, it flows out
Of the doings and fluff
Of our fortunate friends
Who have more than enough.
But when Johnny is hungry
And when Suzie is cold
No one is needing
Of that to be told.

Va—Room! Va—Room!

One hour, I was a little child
Which quickly passed, but in a while
Again, I played those childish games
With my own children much the same.

And now from youth to age and old
The lord has three times blessed my soul.
Yes, once myself and twice as guest
Three times, I count. I have been blessed.

For once again that siren song
Calls, come Grandfather, play along.
And though I make a feigned protest
One can't refuse a favorite guest.

And soon I find I'm on the floor
And toys are scattered door to door.
Had I supposed such times were gone?
Perhaps I did, but I was wrong.

I find a car. she finds one too.
And I reveal what cars can do.
"Cars make noise, "Va—Room!" I say
And then we both Va-Room! away.

November's Wind

The months slip by in ordered line.
August yields to fair September.
October came with its leaves of flame
And worthy to be remembered.

The forest turned from green to gold
And rusty reds and browns.
And from the boughs of every tree
Its finery fluttered down.

The tin roof, on the old wood shed
Bore many an acorn's fall.
They each announced their drop to earth
With a loud and ringing call.

And my wife observed that late each fall
And somewhere near November
A big wind comes and strips away
The adornment from the timber.

And where Autumn hung on by a thread
To trees both small and big,
That howling blow leaves not a sign
On any limb or twig.

And it is not lost on me this year,
That fall has fell on me,
And that I am nearer November now
Then I really care to be.

But with what remains of what was best
I do the best I can.
And like the leaves, I'm holding on
While waiting for the wind.

A Time of Leaving

They are going, a voice was saying.
A long good-bye and they were gone.
Long I stood and looked forlornly
Down the path they traveled on.

Do I see them cross the valley,
Cross the bridge that spans the stream?
In the twilight disappearing
To that misty realm of dreams?

Turning now back to the cabin
Knowing that inside the door
Round the table where we gathered
I shall see their face no more.

More Than Enough

Somewhere near the end of a long journey
In a secluded little vale,
Two foot-weary travelers paused,
      And camped beside the trail.

Hardships cement relationships
And in all things - they shared.
They laughed and talked into night
      As if without a care.

And woke at dawn and packed to break
That cozy little camp
And damped the fire that kept away
      The evenings cool and damp

How are provisions holding out?
Have we enough to do?
Asked one of them. Is there enough
      To see our journey through?

A sadness filled the other's eyes
As gazing down the road
More than enough, the other said
      And shouldered up the load.

July

Pity poor July!
Which has inspired no poet
Some hallowed verse to pen.
A mere stepping stone from spring's bright promise
To fall's brief and short-lived glory.
But that is another story
Not told here.

No, I am thinking more of red juicy ripe tomatoes,
Grapes heavy laden on the vine.
Of cool swimming holes, cane fishing poles,
And the good old summer time.
Of golden, luscious, freestone peaches, pretty girls on
Broad white beaches, and Mom's blackberry wine.

The cacophony of katydids, who overhead
Keep a ragged sort of time
With the fire flies twinkling light
That brightens fields and wooded hills
On balmy summer nights.
Or the creak of chain on a front porch swing
On a Sunday afternoon.
These are just as rare, at least to me
As any day in June

Christmas Present

By my hearth stone on Christmas eve
Our tree is all a-twinkle.
The light falls on my father's hands
Where once was not a wrinkle.

The children's beds are vacant now
Where one time they were sleeping,
Or creeping to the bannister
For Santa Claus a-peeping.

No Christmas stockings now are hung
In hope and expectation,
Which leaves a hole too big to fill
In all our decorations.

And now I hear that it may snow
That Christmas may be white.
But no sweet dreams of sugar plums
Are in this house tonight.

An Unruly Visitor

The big storm came in the waning light of the first day of summer, hastening in the darkness early, stealing the sunset, hushing bird song, bringing wind, rain. Lightning, thunder, and fear traveling in close company.

An unruly visitor was knocking at my door, which I did not have to let in, but could not stop from raging around the house. To retain a calm and steady composure when confronted with such overwhelming power is hard to do. When all your smug self-assurance is carried away with the patio umbrella, when chaos has decided to pay you a visit.

The outside air is quickly churned into a viscous, white, turbulent mist. Thunder drums and the forest, partnered with the wind, becomes trees gone mad, engaging in a wild, frenzied, swaying dance. Rain comes down in sheets, lightning comes down like rain and there is nothing you can do but wait and pray, so wait and pray you do. Then, after a long while, you see the sky brighten just enough to offer hope, and not unlike a ride on a tall, steep, and too fast roller coaster, when the worst is finally over, you feel stirred and uncommonly wonderful! Lord! I truly fear and love your storms.

After the brunt had passed, I pulled up a chair to an upstairs window, sat down and looked out into the fast fading light at the woods surrounding the house. I pulled the sash up to its full height, inviting in the cool, sanitized, and polarized air, and wished the old air out. Then hypnotized, watched the broad backside of the storm waddle away. The lightninig display was short on color and design, but what it lacked in that, it more than made up for in quantity and terror.

Now in comparative safety, no longer between the hammer and the anvil, I watched the flashes backlight the clouds. Saw a brilliant blue-white bolt rend a hairline fracture in the atmosphere, and then leap from cloud to ground. That was close! Way too close! Then, as if caught in a void of suspended time, you cringe and anticipate the crashing sound to come, and come it does. The house quivers and windows rattle in the wake of the blast made by nature, as it closes and repairs rips in the ceiling of the world, hammering and fastening back together, one blow after another, rolling and rolling, farther and farther away. Thunder is truly a plural phenomenon; it never travels alone.

So the storm went on its way, crashing into towns and villages; leaping, mountains and rivers, like a crazy mule I once heard about, who ran over trees, bushes and through fences, who wasn't blind, but just didn't give a hoot. Then a cool and moist stillness blankets the land; the last remnant drops of the storm drip from leaves, down to other leaves, making their pattering way to the forest floor. In the distance the great storm goes grumbling and muttering, off to the South.

Later, about ten thirty that night, it passed out of both sight and hearing. The first storm of summer was over.

Rambling

Bluet's

Mid all the blossoms of the spring I see,
        the Bluet seems the dearest one to me.

For who can name a price or know the worth,
        to bring the blue of sky down to the earth.

As a carpet, wove by nature, they are found,
        to raise a star-crossed bloom above the ground.

Though not as brilliant, as the dogwood, mid the pine,
        still, the spirit of the spring. I think is thine.

For its small and modest nature does impart,
        the message blown within the viewers heart.

That appearing but a moment does attest,
        the bloom of spring is fleeting at its best.

And we shall fade, as Bluets 'neath the grass,
        in hope, as they, that winter time will pass.

Out of Body

By the fireside in my parlor
On a cold December day,
Vacant gazing at the embers
>for my heart was far away.

Far away my heart was flying,
Where transported by its power,
I was racing through a woodland
>at a hundred miles an hour.

Ever Southward, straight and level
Through a land of fragrant pine,
I was standing on the throttle
>I was holding to the line.

Silent spun the constellations
In the night air clear and chill,
And a clarion note was sounding
>from a tower on a hill.

And I saw a little roadster
Speeding off into the night,
I stood and watched its passage
>til it faded out of sight.

Then I was standing by the highway
In the dark and in the gloom,
With a stillness all about me
      like the silence of a tomb.

And I saw this gray-haired fellow
Who was dozing in his chair.
And I saw that he was dreaming
      Of a distant time and hour.

He was dreaming of the spring time
In the pleasant month of May.
He was warming in the sunshine
      on a cold December day.

Forest Smoke

A summer morning in the mountains, the rabbits,
    are making coffee in the woods.

Their little fires they circle round, all tended
    very carefully, as they should.

They tell the story of beginnings as they wait
    for their coffee pots to brew.

The older rabbits tell the story to the younger,
    and it always seems as new.

A tale older than the stones, the mountains,
    the rivers, and grandfather trees,

Of when rabbits were the rulers of the world,
    and how rabbits came to be.

But I do not know that story, only of it,
    nor have I seen their coffee camps.

Only seen the wispy smoke, rising from the forest,
    in the mornings, cool and damp.

Spring Symphony

The frogs creep out of the mud and the mire
And they tell of the coming spring.
Though the air is chill, and the frost still bites,
The frogs have a mind to sing.

From the bog and the pond, and the bank of the creek,
They burp, and they chirp, and they croak.
And their voices blend with the sound of the wind
As it wakes up the sap in the oaks.

Tis a merry sound to the cow and the hound,
To the birds and the beasts together.
Who endured the cold, and coped with the snow
In the hope of the bright spring weather.

So here's to the frog who lives in the bog.
Let's raise him a glass of cheer!
And drink him a toast as the one with the most
Welcome song of the year.

One Stormy Day

Look thee away!
The dark clouds gather in the western sky
And drag their skirts across the high mountain ridges.
And listen thee, to the rumble and the roll of distant thunder
Tumbling through the long cloud valleys
On a boisterous and unseen journey across the sky.
To thee, announcing this heavenly visitor, not to be ignored,
The approaching storm.

Was for thee!
It was born, in the afternoon heat, of this warm spring day
Midwifed by the lofty mountains,
This child of chaos, nourished only by the sun and damp,
Grew both fat and tall in just one hour.
And to those who cower along it's chosen random path,
It brings a blessing, or a curse, or both.

Look thee!
To how it walks across the land on lightning legs.
Burns and blacks each place it steps.
And how ahead the warm air is waked from its doldrum state,
Gathers up itself and rushes to whatever fate
This afternoon may bring.

Look thee and listen!
The day darkens! The birds have stopped singing!
And all the earth grows still and waits.

And then!
It bursting, comes into the woods, with crack and crash.
Each bolt by each flash exposed, and instant rends the air.
The cool rain falls, the wild wind blows!
And hear thee how the mighty thunders roll!
Does it not speak to thee,
That God is in His heaven,
And all the earth still bends unto His will?
And if thee can hear
Tell me true, can thee not also see
A little bit, the storm in me?

Creation's Voice

To yonder cloud-ringed mountains once
      I would go at times.
I trekked from peak to distant peak
      In every season's clime.

Ofttimes I walked in winter's snow
      But oftener in spring
When with the birds, I gloried so,
      My heart was moved to sing.

When all above was blue and cloud
      Ore all the verdant hills,
The flower's sprung, the waters sang,
      In all the rocky rills.

And many a peaceful dream I dreamed
      Beneath the eagle's nest.
And many a dawn I rose to greet
      Upon the mountain's breast.

Where, from the far horizon round,
      Where sky and mountains meet,
The golden sun brought treasure from,
      And dropped it at my feet.

My doubting heart was there rebuked
    By hill and rock and sky.
For one who speaks with such a voice
    Is hard to be denied.

More dumplings

More dumplings!
Cried the old codger king, as he
Sleeve wiped, thin, cracked lip things,
In a kitchen drab and drear,
But Barbie dolls once frolicked here,
Now packed a tangled holocaust
Of dreams done, moments lost,
Box-stored in a dust-dim cranny,
And across from him - sat gray old granny
"Get'um yerself!" She said,
"I'm tired!"

Conformity

I have been caught up as a small pebble
In the flood of humankind.
Swept along with the rush of humanity,
And dragged along the bottom,
Until all the rough edges have worn away,
And I am left smooth and featureless
As are all the old stones,
With whom I take my place,
To wear other stones away.

Voyager

Our atmosphere, how like a roof,
Brave shield of blue and white.
But the illusion ends with the setting sun
For there is no roof at night.

Then is unveiled that boundless reach
We alone can comprehend.
Thy star flung universe unfolds,
Oh, world that has no end.

Arise my soul. above this earth,
Surmount this lonely sphere,
Breakout in space, escape, escape
These chains that bind us here.

Race out beyond the cratered moon,
Slingshot the fiery sun.
But the trek into yon timeless void
Has only just begun.

Be not ensnared by Saturn's rings,
Or the void beyond Pluto.
For no walls exist - no marks define,
The lengths that we can go.

There is no gulf we cannot cross,
No void too great to span,
Within thy universe revealed
To thy God-like third of man.

Undefeated

But I say, a man cannot be called defeated,
Who beaten, but unbowed, has just retreated,
To a higher plane, where he will make a firmer stand,
And there be the more defiant man.

For stand he will, but braver than before,
As one acquainted with the sounds of war,
Who will not quail again before that blast,
Though dying be his gruesome task,

Who believes he has a cause worth dying for.

Troubles

Troubles are like pot holes
    On the road of life.

Those who run too fast
    Or travel in the dark,

It seems to me, are doomed to break
    Both pocketbook and heart.

Reflection

Not as an epiphany,
Nor even yet a thought
But as a remembered fragrance might,
Faint, pleasant, yet undefined,
Create a longing, bittersweet!
To briefly drift across the mind,
But it came to me too quickly,
Triggered by a note of song,
And strung too tight to be unraveled,
Remained unknown,
       and it was gone.

Poets Try

A poet tries to describe a tree
But a poem can never be one
To paint a sunset with adjectives
But a poem will never see one
Or try to rhyme with love and life
But a poem will never live
Still, the poet does the best he can
With what he has to give.
When his soul is washed of longing
Which he takes outside to dry
Both good and bad hang in the sun
And are seen by passers-by.

Barefoot Dream

Go to bed old man
Slip behind the veil
Drive small, quick cars
Climb high, steep trails.

Go bask in the sun
On a white sand beach.
Visit soft-lit bars
On rain dark streets.

Flirt with the girls, then
Ask one to dance.
March with Dr. King, sing,
Give peace a chance.

Hop, rock to rock in
A snow, cold stream.
Go to bed old man
Have a barefoot dream.

If I Had Wings

If I could fly, if I had wings
And as a bird could sail the sky,
Oh, such a song I think I'd sing
If I had wings, if I could fly.

Then all the day, I'd dive and soar
Then rest atop some grand old tree,
Above earths rattle and its roar
Where nothing low could bother me.

The Tribal Council

What is beyond the hills, my Father?
    I do not know, my son.
The sun comes up the sun goes down,
    he has his race to run.

But where goes the sun, my Father?
    He goes to sleep, my son,
And when he rises from his sleep
    a new day is begun.

How gets he to the rising place,
    my Father, tell me true?
He sleeps ore there, but rises here
    does that not bother you?

When I was young it did, my son,
    when I was young as you.
Was many a thing I wondered at
    and sought the answers to.

But learned of stars in heavens sky
    I've only glimpsed a few.
And those which lie beyond my sight
    will never come to view.

Still, it may be in days to come
        someone may find a way
To answer thus and so of things,
        but what of that today?

No Farewell

Youth does not so much die
    as it does - depart the premises.
It begins to take time off; take trips,
    each holiday being longer then the last.
Until one day it will slip away and not return.
    You will have become so accustomed to its presence
That you will not notice it is gone, until another day
    you will look for it and not find the smallest trace.
Then you will stand and wonder where it went,
    and will not know.

Wreck on Turkey Pen Ridge

Quaint and curious that I found,
And miles and miles from any road,
Wheels and gears below the trail
Beside a rusting hulk exposed.

Beneath the laurel and creeping vine,
An accident perhaps, I deemed,
Stripped of parts for spares I'm sure,
A dinosaur from the age of steam.

Lookout, now boys she's about to go!
Somebody might have gave a shout,
Before it fell out of control.
Did the driver go leaping out?

Did it cost that man his job
Or foot, or limb, or worse his life?
How sad a note to carry back
To boss, or home, or waiting wife.

Beneath warm sun and skies of blue,
Beneath leaves turning green to red,
I left the bearer of old news,
The tractor wrecked, the driver's dead.

A Work Not Signed

I took a walk into what was an old abandoned field where every wild seed and root, for a season or two, had an equal chance for survival; which had produced such a wild profusion of growth that any passage through such a strangling tangle had to be carefully chosen. For nature in its slow and steady way was working to heal years of overuse by a passed parade of vanished farmers.

There, deep within, I chanced upon a puzzle of eroded gullies, of crumpled slate and raw red clay, not yet reclaimed by the scrub pine and thorny bramble. And there, by my foot, lay an arrow point, black and shining, lately uncovered by time and the elements, which was too beautifully perfect to have been thrown away by the former owner.

As I retrieved it, I wondered how long it had been since it was held in another hand. And how this place must have looked at the time it was lost and how it came to be here, and if the former owner regretted the loss of this little care-marked stone. Too precious to be lost again, even by me, to whom it was only a curiosity.

So, I imagined some desperate enterprise must have caused the old separation, but if of anger, fear, or hunger, I had no way to know. Perhaps some fatally wounded deer, leaving the hunter far behind, came here to die. Perhaps it lay hidden and bleeding, in the dense undergrowth beneath the shadow of some ancient towering tree, of a shape and size my eyes will never see. Until at last, deer, bone, tree, and the hunter, went the way of all the earth, and of that event and time, only this small hard flint remains.

A work of art, an ancient work not signed, but when and how it came, and who the hunter artist was, are left to musings of the mind; where I see two that talked in a campfire's glow. But what words that were spoke curled around in the smoke and were carried away by the wind.

Winsome Wind

I heard this little winsome wind
That blew in from the sea.
I thought I heard a voice inside
Reciting poetry.

I thought I heard, how sad, how sad
That I have come so far
Not to find one pleasant door
A little bit ajar.

And then the winsome wind withdrew
As winsome winds will do.
And left my door and coming round
Into my window flew.

What means this wind, I said to me,
So rudely to intrude
To in my house so boldly come
Disturbing solitude.

To which the winsome wind replied
Still whispering in short verse,
I came to bring a blessing
But now I shall leave a curse.

I curse the door, I curse the house
I curse the window, too.
And having cursed them all complete
I last of all curse you.

To dream in rhyme, to think in rhyme
To write in rhyming, too.
Thus said the wind from that day on
I was condemned to do.

Then whispered it around my head
What seemed a long, long time.
It took the whispering when it left
But did not take the rhyme.

And so it is with poets mad
Cursed by a winsome wind
Who should have left their window closed
And never let it in.

Sail Away

My little boat, serenely floats
At the end of a long quiet dock.
And on the waves of a balmy tide
It gently bobs and rocks.

The Zephyr of a morning breeze
Plays in among the spars,
And raps the lines against the mast
For countless hours and hours.

It's not too long, nor short a boat
And rigged just right for me,
So I could sail her all alone
Should I ever put to sea.

It is an old recurring dream
I dreamed again today.
I climbed aboard my trusty craft
And quietly sailed away.

Where I am bound, I do not know
The dream it does not say
I only know, I step aboard
And simply sail away.

The Evening and the Morning

The Evening and the Morning once
      did meet upon the way.
The Evening full of lessons learned
      had many a thing to say.
Of heat of sun, of storms that come,
      of how the winds may blow.
He told the Morning all the things
      he thought he'd need to know.

The Evening spoke his final thoughts
      on all those things he knew.
And done with that, he tipped his hat
      and Morning bid adieu.

The Morning armed with sound advice
      went on his way alone.
He hitched his pants, he set his face,
      and made himself at home.

Seeker of Fortune

Farewell to the seeker of fortune.
        Godspeed and luck to you!
Though sad it is for those you loved
        to bid you fond adieu.

For all those haunts and places
        where we good friends before
Would laugh and raise a glass of cheer
        will see your face no more.

Your house is empty and forlorn,
        its rooms and walls are bare.
The windows where your light would shine
        now have a vacant stare.

For you're gone to seek your fortune,
        with a Howdy! Ho! And Hey!
And far across the gladden fields
        and down the road away.

L. Clayton Cate

Roses, Quilts, and Time

Behold the noble poet.
He sits with ink and pen,
Puts down a line then draws it through,
And fits a new one in.

He makes a quilt created of
Metaphors and rhyme
So we may know
Love bloomed a rose
Within the poets mind.

I applaud thee, master poet,
With thee I shed a tear.
Thy window glows far in the dark
Across the vanished years.

Thy love and rose combining with
A briar of thorny root,
That love could cause
A heart to bleed.
It has the ring of truth.

Westward Trek

*The inspiration for this poem came from
a day hike to Silars Bald in 1984.*

This is as far as I dare go.
I must return or lose the light.
For I came ill prepared this day
To find my way at night.

But in the distance, I can see
The trail goes on and on.
And I am sad, I must turn back,
With bare a half day gone.

L. Clayton Cate

For looking on from this high perch
Along the lofty crest,
A sea of rolling mountain tops
March off into the west.

I can make out on a distant rise
There winding through the heath,
A path that goes among the clouds
With all the world beneath.

And there a westward traveler goes
With a brightly colored pack,
Content I'm sure that all he needs
He carries on his back.

God speed! Adventurous soul, I thought
As he disappeared from view
My body turns my feet around
My heart is gone with you.

Walking Softly

Wake!
Light seeps into the darkness
On the eastern rim of sky.
The harbinger of day that comes
When things of night must fly.
Sans stars, sans moon and all their kind
For the sun is coming
And brings its shine.

Time enough, and time
To break this camp, to make an end.
To strike this tent
That was my shelter from the wind.
To quench the flame that cooked my bread.
To roll the blanket
That was my bed.

Time, time to be done
Before that light is fully come.
Conceal the remnants of the fire
Where once was kindled heart's desire.
Sweep leaves and twigs
On marks and tracks.
I was not here.
I will not be back.

New Tenant

A tree fell in the forest.
It did not bend but broke.
And light rushed in
And filled the space,
Vacated by the oak.

Only one

Bright galaxies, far flung through space
Must number in the millions.
And worlds like mine, it may well be
Exist perhaps in billions.
Stars to behold, on cloudless nights
Far more than eye can see.
So many, many, there are of them
But only one...of me

No One More Than Me

There were two ships that met at sea.
The younger you, the elder me.
Two ships that met at sea.

Our course the same, for leagues a few,
Then west for me, then south for you.
It was the south for you.

Then out beyond the leeward rail
I watched your fast receding sail.
Your white receding sail.

I stood, I wished, as days shall pass,
Fair wind for you, more than you ask,
Much more than you might ask.

Till anchored safe in port you lie,
No one shall wish that more than I,
No, no one more than I.

O troubled world, O storm wrought sea,
No one shall want that more than me,
No, no one more than me.

Where Blue Mountains Are

Perhaps upon some vaulted crest
Where air is bright and sweet,
I'll go and claim myself a view
Then find myself a seat.

And gaze across a rolling sea
Of wave on wave of green
And think on all the hills I've climbed
And all the in-betweens.

And far away a valley is
And far below me, too.
And all above is lighted with
The fairest shade of blue.

And there a shining river is,
With wooded ridge beyond.
After that blue mountains are
And after that the dawn.

Go Out, Young Man!

Go out, young man, upon the road
That passes nearly by.
Go out, look on the travelers there.
Go, look them in the eye.

Go tell them you are searching truth,
A stranger to these parts.
Then look upon their puzzled state
And deep into their hearts.

A shallow face they show to you
Concerning what you seek.
They are like ghosts upon the road,
Who long have been asleep.

Then come back here and tell me, son,
And drink with me a round.
And we shall laugh and raise a toast
No matter what you found.

The Cowboy Way

Somewhere in the great Southwest, in the cool of the eve-n'n, the ranch hands are resting on the bunk house porch. The new hand (a young fellow) has asked about the lone grave down by the creek he passed riding in. The top-hand relates this story about the man whose grave it is.

That old cowpoke came riding in
Dust covered hat to tail,
With the western sky all bloody red
And light about to fail.

Seen him coming in the distance,
When he topped that little rise,
A silhouette of man and pony
Moving dark a'gin the sky.

His little pony was coming easy
In a slow and gentle gait.
Must have known where he was going
Fer he didn't hesitate.

Come and stopped before the bunkhouse,
Standing, holding down his head,
We were slow to come to guess it,
That his rider, he was dead.

Cause, he sat there in the saddle.
With that sorta grace o' form,
That a man don't get from learn'n
It's the way that he was born.

And the evening turn'n purple
Lent an eerie kinda charm
To that cowboy in the saddle
With a death grip on the horn.

With his skin all burnt and wrinkled,
And his face as hard as flint,
With his hands all gnarled and calloused,
And his finger bones all bent.

That look that comes from outdoor livin',
From a life spent on the range,
Playing nurse to maverick cattle,
Be it sun, or snow, or rain.

So we eased him off his pony,
laid him down there in the yard,
Still a sitt'n on his saddle cause
He gripped that horn so hard.

S'pose it sounds a tad bit funny,
Man and saddle on the ground.
But. nobody wasn't laugh'n
We just stood a star'n down.

I don't know what they were think'n
But, an educated guess
Is that dy'in in the saddle
Was a cowboy kinda test.

Well, we buried him next morning
'Neath that willow, by the creek,
Still a sitting on his saddle,
So we put him good and deep.

With oratory by the boss man,
He come and said a little word,
It was short and sad and pointed,
But the best l ever heard.

Some-thin' bout a coming morning.
Some-thin' bout a time of rest.
But that part 'bout heaven's prairies
Was the part I liked the best.

No, he didn't have no coffin,
Just the blanket from his roll,
But we did a part'n gesture
'Fore we covered up the hole.

Ferd, he thought he'd need a neck tie,
Lundy thought a bar of soap,
But we all pitched in together
Fer a brand new throw'n rope.

And that's the way we done it.
Buried saddle, man, and gun,
Sent that pony he was ride'n
Running free, beneath the sun.

Then we raised that little marker
Has a date but not a name
So you'd never know by look'n
Bout the reason for his fame.

But when you pass that feller's grave,
Son, you ought to tip your hat
For as a cowboy way of dying
Ain't nobody topp'n' that.

www.ingramcontent.com/pod-product-compliance
Lightning Source LLC
Chambersburg PA
CBHW060353080526
44583CB00012B/289